MW01595210

ANNE BONNY

A Novel By

Stephen Utley

ANNE BONNY

A Novel by

Stephen Utley

U.S. Copyright Registration Number 1-737-803-961

WGAW Registered 1433385

www.annebonnythenovel.com

10 9 8 7 6 5 4 3 2 1

First Edition © 2012 by Stephen Utley

ISBN: 978-1480066854

All rights reserved. No part of this story may be used or reproduced by any means—graphically, electronically, or mechanically, including photocopying, recording, or taping, or by any information storage retrieval system without the written permission of the author except in the case of brief quotations embodied in critical articles and reviews.

Because of the dynamic nature of the Internet, any Web addresses or links contained within this work may have changed since original publication and may no longer be valid.

Certain characters in this work are historical figures, and certain events portrayed within this work actually took place. However, this is a work of fiction. All of the characters, names and events as well as places, incidents, organizations, and dialogue in this novel either are the products of the author's imagination or are used fictitiously.

DEDICATION

I dedicate this story to the memory of John and Jimmy, my oldest and youngest brothers who left us too early in life.

CONTENTS

ACKNOWLEDGMENTS

I thank my family and friends for their encouragement and support that helped me stay focused on continuing my journey and to take my thoughts further than I imagined.

To Shannon. Had she not convinced me to attend a historical lecture aboard a cruise ship sailing through the Caribbean, I would have never heard the story of Anne Bonny.

To Amy for helping me better understand aspects of the story from woman's perspective and for assisting with the final stages of publishing Anne Bonny.

A special thanks to all who graciously contributed their valuable time to make this a better story.

Last but not least, a special thanks to the grey-haired professor who spun a tale of vivid history, marvelous characters, challenging circumstances, the unknown forces and impact of nature and the classic, timeless themes of literature that are the hallmarks of a captivating and riveting story.

.

CHAPTER ONE

AN ARGUMENT IN THE NIGHT

It's a cold autumn night in our year of the lord 1700, inside a small home on the outskirts of County Cork, Ireland. Shadows of two figures cast from oil lamps shift erratically with agitated movements as a heated argument takes place. The sounds of muffled voices can be heard. As the volume of the voices peaks, the home's large front door swings open, slamming hard against the cottage's limestone exterior. William Cormac steps outside, leaving the door open, and walks briskly up the stone and mortar path.

Struggling with his coat, he suddenly pauses, turns back to face his home, takes one step back and stops. A sudden cold wind hits him, sending a chill through his body. He pulls his loose-fitting coat tighter and shakes his head as if the wind blew away any clouded thought he may have had of going back. Peering back through the still-open door, he sees the warm yellow-orange glow flickering from the flames of the candles and lamps. The house is silent now, except for the sounds of his wife, Rachael, sobbing quietly.

As he stands chilled in the brisk breeze, confusing thoughts wage a silent war in his mind. Cormac cannot determine which of his emotions is making him feel worse, the remorse he feels for betraying his wife's trust, or that others will soon learn that he is an adulterer. He knows one thing is certain; his weakness for other women has caused the warmth emanating from his home to be deceiving. His actions have removed any future possibilities of his home ever feeling warm again. His wife will never forgive him—reconciliation is now out of the question. He also knows that if he leaves, he can never return.

He turns away from the home and with a deliberate pace begins walking toward the stables. Minutes later, the sound of a horse's harsh cry pierces the night's calm as Cormac's sharp spurs rake against the horse's flanks, and the animal bolts from the barn.

Tonight, William Cormac's habitual philandering has finally caught up with him. His previous indiscretions had been carefully concealed and mutually secretive—as adultery during this era is considered a serious assault against the sanctity of matrimony—perhaps the most serious offense a man—or woman—could commit.

Rachael has not only discovered his most recent affair with their maid, Mary Brennan, but also now knows the affair has brought forth a child, an illegitimate child. For the disgrace her husband has brought upon her and their home, Rachael has made it clear that she will not rest until all in County Cork know that her husband has committed adultery and has sired a bastard child. She plans to tell everyone that a habitual liar of his sort can never be trusted. She wants her pound of flesh, and will have it by watching William's trusted reputation as a counselor crumble into a million tiny pieces as the result of his actions. With his world falling apart before him, he knows only one place to seek solace. He rides hard into the night to be at Mary's bedside as she struggles through the pain of childbirth. Four hours later, they are the parents of a beautiful baby girl. They will name her Anne.

CHAPTER TWO

CHRISTINE'S MISFORTUNE

With business shrewdness, and his former life left behind, William Cormac begins a new life with Mary and Anne. He decides that the best way to pursue a fresh start is to leave his ravaged life behind in Ireland and secure passage aboard a ship bound for America, Charles Towne, Carolina. There he establishes an export trade business that quickly flourishes. Over the course of a decade, he becomes quite wealthy and purchases a large estate north of the city.

William loves his only child dearly and takes great pains to ensure that Anne receives the finest tutoring—both in terms of formal education and in the social graces. Anne excels, and it is soon obvious to all that she will mature to become a woman of fine standing in the genteel society of the South.

Everyone acquainted with the Cormac family realizes that

Anne is gifted in many ways. She is not only intelligent, but her unique beauty and deep red hair serve to separate her quickly from other girls her age. As she matures, her womanly features draw the attention of both men and women. Her natural sensuality captures the minds of men, young and old. They see her as an intriguing object of desire and want her. Other women, who travel in high circles, see her as an object of envy. During Anne's early teens, a steady line of young men seeks her company, showing up on the Cormac's porch to leave a calling card.

However, William Cormac allows suitors from only the most prominent families to pay their respects. If their family lineage and social standing are impressive enough, then they could—with a bit of luck—be granted permission to enter into a well-supervised courtship. All is set for Anne to enjoy a life of leisure and comfort. Those closest to her also understand that she has a dark secret: the one thing that she cannot escape and the one thing that people have a difficult time understanding about her. That is Anne's terrible and unpredictable temper, not the type of temper that is easily dismissed. Her raging episodes greatly disturb the people who witness them.

One early morning when Anne is thirteen years old, she wakes from a deep sleep and rises from her large, ornate bed, picks out one of her favorite spring dresses and begins the arduous task of putting on the layers of clothes—constricting corsets and heavily laced underclothes required for young women of her day. While dressing, she glances at her dresser and notices that the bottle of her favorite perfume appears to be nearly empty, containing much less perfume than she remembered from just the day before. *Christine*, Anne says to herself in a sharp, nearly audible whisper. Jumping to a conclusion, she suspects their housemaid, Christine, has stolen her perfume while performing her daily cleaning.

Eighteen-year-old Christine had been hired just six months earlier by William Cormac. During those six months, she has gone about her work and minded her own affairs. On several occasions, she has witnessed Anne's spontaneous tirades and decides, early on, that it would be in her best interest to minimize her contact, keeping her distance from the young woman as much as possible. Anne perceives her distancing as rudeness and quickly decides that she does not like Christine. Now, without hesitation, with the perfume bottle in hand as proof of thievery, Anne storms down the stairs to the kitchen, where she knows that Christine will be preparing breakfast, enters the kitchen and demands a confession.

"You! Why did you steal from me? Did you think that I would not notice my perfume gone? Did you think that I would not notice that just yesterday the bottle was more than half-full?"

Christine is stunned by Anne's accusation and aggressive behavior and adamantly denies the claim. "Lady Cormac, I know not what you are referring to. I would not, and did not steal from you. I am sorry, but you are quite mistaken—I assure you!"

Anne continues to drill her relentlessly, demanding a confession as she shouts only inches from Christine's face, "You were in my room, you stole my perfume, and you know it. Stop lying to me! Speak the truth!"

Christine cannot take the abuse that is being forced upon her. She turns to Anne and says, "I will not stand here and be falsely accused. Your inquisition is that of an insane person and I would not touch your perfume for fear of smelling like a wet dog."

In an instant, Anne's face transforms from that of an unreasonable and agitated woman to that of a crazed Banshee. At this moment, Christine realizes that what she has said may have cost her more than her position at the Cormac estate. Seeing Anne's rage erupting before her, she realizes that she could very well meet physical harm. Anne's anger has moved beyond the point of no return. As she stares into Christine's eyes, a bead of sweat flows from her forehead and down onto her cheek, and she mumbles, as if in a psychotic trance, "Insane? Wet dog!"

The early morning sunlight streams through the kitchen's bay window, causing a sharp reflection temporarily to steal Anne's vision. Christine notices Anne is distracted momentarily and her attention shifts to the reflection. Simultaneously, their eyes land on a silver kitchen knife lying on the table, only feet away.

Without hesitation, Anne leans toward the table, grabs the knife and hears Christine yell, "No!" Anne turns sharply and plunges the six-inch blade into Christine's stomach. The shock of the blade entering her body, combined with the force of Anne's assault, causes Christine to step backward until she collides with the kitchen wall. Anne, still in the midst of her psychotic episode, revels in Christine's submission. She looks into Christine's eyes, which are wide open and staring straight ahead. She only realizes what she has done when she hears her father thundering into the kitchen and yelling frantically, "Annie, Stop! Leave her be!"

Only hours after the incident, William conjures a tale in his parlor, and persuades Christine's father to trade exposure for a sizeable sum of money—a sturdy wooden cigar box filled with the gold coins of the Realm. With this arrangement in place, William manages to keep what has happened private, spinning Christine's injury as an unfortunate accident. Christine's father agrees to stand by the story's accuracy as he is handed the heavy cigar box.

Anyone who inquires is told that Christine has taken an unfortunate spill in the Cormac's kitchen while preparing the family's morning meal. She held a knife in her hand and, striding across the damp kitchen floor, fell awkwardly upon it. All heard Christine cry out as the blade penetrated her stomach.

CHAPTER THREE

NO OTHER CHOICE

Three years have passed since the morning Anne nearly took Christine's life. Anne is now sixteen years of age and has blossomed into a formidable woman. Her body is that of a woman in her twenties. William often reminds her that God has blessed her with uncommon beauty. She also realizes that a watchful God has bestowed upon her another gift—her father's innate understanding of human nature—particularly an understanding of the male half of the species.

All of the eligible young suitors in Carolina pursue her, and they come calling in force. William wants the most for his daughter and will not allow just any young man to be introduced to her. All prospective suitors are scrutinized carefully and must meet his rigid criteria. Anne adamantly opposes the fact that her father has taken complete control of selecting who may or may not be considered a suitable man for her. In her stubborn mind, she is perfectly capable of doing that herself and questions what she believes to be a ridiculous old world tradition.

After a number of visits from several young, eligible men, Anne quickly notices that her beauty and intellect are a powerful combination that, used in just the right way and at the right time, has the power to overwhelm them. She realizes that, at this age, all young men are at a huge disadvantage; their minds are clouded by fantasies of her shedding her clothes and surrendering her body to them. Anne knows that their raging hormones undoubtedly give her the upper hand. They become as trained pups at the beck and call of a skillful handler. She uses this knowledge to manipulate their thoughts and actions—like a puppeteer with mannequins on strings—and enjoys playing mind games during their conversations. Although she enjoys the attention they stumble all over themselves to bestow upon her, she is not at all interested in nervous young boys who are played and intimidated so easily.

One warm and sunny summer day, a courier delivers a message to the Cormac estate. William reads the formal introduction letter sent to him by a wealthy plantation owner named Patrick Wilkinson. The Wilkinson family name is known throughout the South. The letter is brief, succinct, and to the point. It reads:

"Mister Cormac, It is my honor to take this opportunity to formally introduce myself. My name is Patrick Wilkinson. It is my

understanding that you are the proud father of the lovely and inspiring Anne Cormac. With only the best of intentions assured, I respectfully request your permission for my eldest son, Jonathan, who is at present nineteen years old, to travel to Charles Towne and visit your estate to call upon Anne so that he might introduce himself to her. He will, of course, be accompanied by a chaperone of your choosing. Please respond to inform me if this arrangement is acceptable to you and provide me with the first possible date on which Anne—whose reputation for charm, beauty, elegance and grace have spread throughout the region—and Jonathan may be formally introduced."

The letter is signed "With the utmost respect, Your Most Obedient and Humble Servant, Patrick Wilkinson, Charles Towne, Carolina.

William sends a note back agreeing to the introduction. The opportunity to merge the Cormac family with the Wilkinson would elevate each to a position unreachable on its own. Three days later, as planned, Jonathan Wilkinson arrives at the white-painted and arched portal at the front entrance to the Cormac estate. When Anne sees Jonathan for the first time, peering around a corner down the broad spiral staircase, she is immediately awestruck by his masculine features and physical stature. He looks and sounds like a grown man—unlike the others who have come before. The two spend their closely chaperoned afternoon together, talking and laughing. Before leaving, Jonathan shakes William's hand and graciously thanks him for his hospitality. Then, he turns to face Anne, and taking her hand, he surreptitiously slips her a small, folded note.

With a bow and click of his well-polished boot heels, Jonathan Wilkinson, one of the most eligible—and desired— bachelors in the southern colonies, turns and boldly strides out the door to his waiting carriage.

Anne goes directly to her room to read Jonathan's note. With eager hands and in her haste, she nervously opens the fine parchment:

"Dearest Anne, Let us continue our time together this eve under the moonlit sky. I will be waiting for you at midnight in the gazebo behind your home." Taking a short breath, Anne is startled by the directness—every bit the type of man she desires. She assesses the situation and ponders the likelihood that her father will catch the two of them.

She laughs silently at the idea of being caught. She knows her father's nightly ritual, which consists of poring over his business documents, followed by four well-measured glasses of England's finest gin and a deep sleep on his favorite large parlor chair. He will be oblivious to a clandestine meeting such as that proposed by the brash Mr. Wilkinson.

Lying in bed, Anne listens to the grandfather clock in the hallway at the head of the stairs and impatiently waits for time to pass. In her bedroom, lit only by one tiny candle, she stares at the vaulted ceiling. She watches the dancing flame flickering on the candle on the nightstand and begins to map out possible scenarios for the pending midnight rendezvous. She cannot believe that a man, no matter how handsome, could make her feel the nervous tension she now feels.

Gazing across her room, watching as the candle casts shadows across the walls, she begins to scan the titles of books on the bookshelf nearby her bed. One title immediately catches her eye—Shakespeare's *Romeo and Juliet*. She thinks to herself, *how apropos*, and sarcastically scoffs. She hears the familiar sound of the large grandfather clock beginning to chime the Westminster lead-in to the midnight count. She thinks it odd that she hears the chimes so clearly, after having learned to ignore them for so many years.

Lying back on her bed, Anne considers the choreography and timing of the rendezvous. She does not want to arrive at the gazebo early or on time. The last thing she wants is to appear too eager. Ten minutes after midnight should do. Her skin begins to tingle as though thousands of ants are crawling on her body. Her thoughts progress from the moment of her arrival to fanaticizing about how it will feel to be held against Jonathan's body and for their lips to meet.

At eight minutes after midnight, Anne quietly leaves her home and walks across the beautifully manicured yard toward the gazebo. She sees a shadow—Jonathan waiting for her, and then hears him say in a low voice, "Anne, over here!" As she steps into the gazebo, their lustful thoughts immediately take over and their bodies become as finely intertwined as the marlinspike lines aboard a sailing ship.

Anne has never kissed anyone so passionately before, and is both exhilarated and frightened. She quickly realizes that she is not in control of her situation. The unfamiliar feeling causes a wave of panic to wash over her and she makes an effort to pull away. Recognizing that she may not have a say in the matter, Anne suddenly yells, "Stop!" Jonathan stops for only a second to glance briefly into Anne's frightened eyes, and then laughs and continues on with his by-now unwanted advances. Held tightly by his muscular arms, Anne realizes that she is powerless against him and that she could be in serious trouble. She yells in an angry and authoritative voice, "Jonathan, No more ... please ... stop this now!"

Anne's angry plea only excites Jonathan more, and he intensifies his passionate attack. He pulls Anne against him even tighter and begins squeeze her breasts. Her feeling of helplessness begins to feed her mounting temper, pushing it past its breaking point. Her face turns as red as her fiery hair and her body begins to sweat profusely. She cannot pull away from him—she is locked in a bear hug-like grip—so she improvises. Anne relaxes her body to imply that she has given in to his advances. Anne's trick works, Jonathan, thinking that she has begun to cooperate, relaxes his tight grip on her. At just the right moment, she pulls her arm away and sinks her fingernails deep into his cheek, raking them downward in a swift motion, carving four deep furrows in the flesh. The move catches Jonathan off guard.

Not completely comprehending what has just happened to him, or the loving warmth he had been led to believe he would receive, he reacts to the sudden and intense pain and grabs his cheek as blood begins to flow from the wounds. In a state of shock, he steps back from Anne and lets out a frightened yell. Anne, true to her nature, has already gained the upper hand. Before he has time to react, Anne kicks him in the groin with all her might. Jonathan immediately doubles over, drops to his knees, and releases a long, soulful and painful groan. Anne unleashes a kicking frenzy on Jonathan's flanks as he rolls from side-to-side in an attempt to protect his ribs and head—in addition to the Wilkinson family jewels—from her vicious attack.

When Anne is too exhausted to continue, she finally stops and realizes that Jonathan is no longer moving. He is either unconscious or dead. She is satisfied with either result.

Anne takes a deep breath to compose herself. She wipes the sweat from her face and begins to walk confidently and briskly back to her home to shake her father to life and tell him that Jonathan lies injured on the gazebo floor. William is awakened from a sound sleep to the sight of his daughter sobbing at his bedside. He's half-asleep and confused about what she is telling him, but soon gains enough wit to know that something terrible has happened.

As he heads toward the broad expanse of lawn behind his estate, he summons two house servants at the top of his voice, telling them to meet him at the gazebo—and to rush. When he sees Jonathan's unconscious body with four deep stripes of blood dripping from his face, he yells, "Annie, go to your room *now* and wait for me there." Anne pauses for a brief moment, glaring at Jonathan's motionless body. Kneeling next to Jonathan and viewing the scene in the light of a lamp carried by one of the servants, William looks at Anne and yells in a voice rarely used, "Now Annie. I said to leave now!"

He sends a servant to fetch a physician ten miles away toward the center of town. An hour later, Jonathan Wilkinson is transported by carriage to the small clinic attached to the doctor's home where he will remain for the next two weeks recovering from the concussion, contusions, and broken ribs that resulted from Anne's ferocious beating.

William is at his wit's end with Anne. He sits in his parlor mulling over the reasons why his daughter exhibits such violent behavior and recalls that he first noticed the changes in her behavior—the latent aggressiveness—just as she entered her early teen years. At two o'clock in the morning, once the excitement had died down and all is once again quiet at the Cormac estate, William walks to the base of the staircase and yells, "Annie, come down here this instant. I need to have a word with you."

Anne is lying awake in her bed when she hears her father's voice. She opens her bedroom door and responds, "Coming, father." She walks down the stairs expecting to see her father at the base of the staircase, his arm outreached and his firm hand gripping the banister, but he is not there. She proceeds to the parlor, just off the main hall inside the front doors and sees him seated on the large overstuffed chair near his fireplace. His head is down and his elbows rest on his knees—the better to keep his hands from shaking.

He looks at her and slowly says, "Annie, sit down." Anne

sits in a matching chair across from him. William leans back and stares at Anne for a moment before asking, "Annie, what could have possibly happened between you and the Wilkinson boy that could have caused him to leave here in such a condition?"

"Father, that boy deceived me. As he left us earlier, he handed me a secret note telling me that he had an urgent matter to discuss with me; a matter of life and death!"

"I don't understand. What could be a matter of life and death, Annie? Do you still have this note? I would like to see it."

"No Father. I do not know where it is."

"Think hard Annie. How could this note have simply disappeared? Where did you see it last?"

"I had the note with me when I left my room to meet with Jonathan at midnight at the gazebo. I suppose he took it from me when he attacked me!"

"Did you say he attacked you? Annie, look at me—this is of the utmost importance. You said the Wilkinson boy attacked you? Did he harm you? I do not see a mark on you, nor does your clothing appear to be torn or crumpled."

Anne begins to shed forced tears—an art she had mastered in childhood—and says, "Father, he tried to take what is not his ... he tried to have his way with me." Anne covers her face with her hands and begins to elevate the intensity of her acting.

"Annie, how did the Wilkinson boy receive his wounds?"

Anne had anticipated the question and was quick with the answer. "Father, when he held me and would not let me go, I pushed him away and he took a terrible fall."

William desperately wants to believe his daughter, but he is suspicious of Anne's story from the start. He considers that she is fabricating it and shedding tears to play upon his emotions to cloud his reasoning. Over the years, he has come to know when he is being played. He senses that feeling now.

He rises from his chair and begins to pace slowly around the room. "You say Jonathan fell? Maybe you can tell me how many times he fell?"

"How many times? I do not understand your question. Father, I feared for my life. Jonathan was forcing himself upon me and would not stop no matter what I said. I cannot recall such details. The last thing I remember is that I began to panic and as I broke free, I pushed him and he fell awkwardly. It all happened so fast."

"Daughter, if the Wilkinson boy received his wounds from falling, I would estimate that he must have fallen a minimum of ten to fifteen times, and from a higher vantage point than the deck of the gazebo. And tell me, how did he receive the four deep scratches on his face?"

Anne replies, sensing that her foolproof, never fail grip on her father's logic was slipping on this occasion. "Father, why the inquisition? You act as though you do not believe your own daughter!" She holds her hands over her face and delivers a convincing sob—complete with tears.

Anne draws inward now, working naively to conjure up a scheme that will assure her father that she is telling the truth. She does not realize that she is no match for his experiences with human nature—especially when he suspects a rat in the woodpile. Drawing upon his days as a barrister in Ireland, when William Cormac listened to guilty people lie to him, perjuring themselves while delivering testimony or during cross-examination, he watches Anne.

Over time, he acquired a talent for instantly sensing a lie coming his way. Likewise, Anne's story is so absurd—*prima facie*—at first glance—that William easily sees it for what it is. He quickly reconstructs a hypothetical situation in his mind that he believes likely took place and says, "Annie, I will tell you what I presume took place. When you first laid eyes on Jonathan, you were taken by his square jaw and his polite, but playful, demeanor. Before the end of the day, you were curious ... no, you were more than curious, you were infatuated with him. You began to see the manly side of him.

"He may indeed have given you a secret note. However, I am sure that it had nothing to do with life or death. It was more than likely an encouragement for you to meet him in the gazebo later in the evening for a romantic interlude," he injected for rhetorical emphasis. "You put yourself in a precarious situation, and when he had you in his clutches you became frightened, somehow gained an upper hand and then beat him ..."

Anne interrupts her father. "It upsets me that my own father, my own flesh and blood, does not believe me." Anne began to pour on the loving father/daughter tactic—it has almost always been guaranteed to work. "It bothers me to no end that, for some reason, you always think yourself smarter than others. You were not there as I was attacked and, unless I've missed something, you have never possessed the ability to peer into the past. You act as though you think me a harlot!"

"Annie, I will no longer stand for your lies and brazen disrespect for me. Your volatile temper and your recurring acts of violence are out of control and they are continual thorns in my side. You have come close to killing two people. Three years ago, it was Christine, and now poor Jonathan Wilkinson, a fine gentleman whom you beat to a bloody pulp and within an inch of his life. You must find a way to …"

Anne again interrupts her father. "Poor Jonathan … poor Jonathan! Old man, you know nothing of what you speak."

"Annie, I don't care if you are a young woman of sixteen. If you continue to speak to me in this manner, I will find a suitable hickory switch and beat you into submission as I would a young lad who disrespects the word of his father."

"So now you want to beat me into submission. Father, I think that it is clear to both of us from where my temper comes. It is obvious that you have passed your own flaws on to me."

Infuriated, William raises his voice to be heard throughout the halls. "Enough!" he says. "Enough!"

Anne simply rises from her chair, walks out of the parlor,

and stomps up the stairs to her bedroom.

Once again, William is faced with having to clean up Anne's mess. That morning, he visits both the doctor who treated Jonathan and the driver who transported him to the clinic in town. He pays the doctor five quid and the driver two for a slight alteration of the night's events.

While visiting both doctor and driver, William simply says, "I appreciate that you have taken time to meet with me on such short notice. I will get straight to the point. I need to ask a favor of you." As he looks them in the eye, he hands each a sealed envelope with a clearly outlined bulk in the form of paper currency enclosed.

The carriage driver says nothing and accepts the envelope without question. The doctor looks at the envelope and asks, "Mister Cormac, what might this be?" William and the carriage driver momentarily lock eyes. It is obvious to William that the carriage driver has accepted hush money before. The carriage driver uncomfortably looks away without saying a word. William replies, "Only a small token of my appreciation for both the valuable services you provided at a time of dire need. I am truly grateful for your assistance earlier and need your help to recreate the series of events that found young Jonathan in the care of the hospital where he lies comfortably.

"Since Jonathan had visited my home earlier that day, I was disturbed when I learned that he was so brutally attacked. I was told that at approximately midnight an anonymous and concerned citizen found Jonathan face down and unconscious in an alley near the docks in Charles Towne, an apparent victim of vagrants attempting to rob him of his possessions.

The robbery was foiled and the perpetrators fled the scene. When asked to identify himself, Jonathan, in a semi-conscious state, uttered the Cormac name. Being unknown in this area, he was therefore brought back to my estate. Doctor, that was the very moment that I sent for you, where you then treated and had Jonathan transported to your clinic to receive uninterrupted attention and to undergo any specialized treatment he may need."

"Doctor, I will need you to keep a careful watch over Jonathan and inform him how lucky he is to be amongst the living this morning. I will also need you to inform him of what happened and how he ultimately found himself a patient under your care. If he should make other claims as to what he believes happened to him, you are to inform him that the severe beating he received during the attempted robbery has caused him to have delusions. I will then visit him myself this afternoon to reinforce what happened to him and to inform him that I have contacted his father and sent word by the speediest available means that he is safe and being well cared for."

Cormac then asks each man to repeat the story back to him, listens to them, and seals the pact with a shake of each hand.

CHAPTER FOUR

THE ANGEL OF CHARLES TOWNE

Anne's mother has fallen ill with a fever, and William, continually by her bedside, gives her words of encouragement. Only the finest doctors attend to her. However, after six days, she takes a sudden, unexplainable downturn and late in the afternoon, quietly passes away.

William, neither understanding nor expecting the sudden loss of the love of his life, sinks into a deep depression and drinks heavily for over two months. Luckily, William's business is well established and in the good hands of his business partner while he mourns. The duties of maintaining the Cormac estate fall squarely to Anne and their regular staff. She has been waited on her whole life and finds transitioning into her new role of running their home difficult. However, with the help of others, she manages the estate's matters successfully.

The responsibilities that now occupy her time are also a blessing, taking her thoughts away from the loss of her caring and doting mother.

One day, after several weeks have passed, a prominent Charles Towne family sends an invitation asking William and Anne to attend a gala. Anne looks at this invitation as an opportunity to get her father out of their home, if only for one evening. Society expects a suitable time for grieving, but Anne knows what would be best for her father and graciously accepts the invitation on behalf of them both.

At six o'clock in the evening, on the day of the affair, their horse-drawn carriage is waiting on the pebble-covered circular drive at the front edifice of their sprawling home. William and Anne sit in silence inside the carriage as the driver delivers a quick whistle and a pop on the reins, prompting the two large and well-bred brown horses to move along. Anne looks over and smiles at her father, hoping to entice a smile in return. In lieu of a smile, William Cormac reaches over to gently pat the back of Anne's white-gloved hand.

On their way to the gala, they roll past the bustling and ship-filled port of Charles Towne before entering the streets of the commerce district, where the gala is to take place. This is the peak season when merchant ships are anchored offshore or tied securely to the docks, while deckhands and dockworkers frantically transfer the contents of each cargo-laden hold to the vast expanses of the city's warehouses.

The cobblestone streets are crowded at this time of day with a mixed bunch, ranging from well-groomed, well-to-do businessmen waiting for their valuable goods to be unloaded and delivered to their destinations for payment, to rough, toothless, hardworking sailors put ashore to spend their wages on food, hard drink, and as much debauchery as their meager wages will procure.

As their carriage passes the docks, William leans over, gently squeezing his daughter's hand and says, "Annie, take a good look at the many varied souls who have played an integral role in helping to build merchant trade in Charles Towne. We owe them much gratitude, for without these seamen and dockworkers I would not have been able to grow my business." After the shortest of pauses, he continues, "And we would not be leading the comfortable lives we have grown so accustomed to." A broad smile spreads across his face—the first in many a week.

"I am looking, father. I have seen all sorts—an interesting assortment of well-to-do citizens and the most unsavory types of characters."

Anne's father did not have to ask her to look; she has been looking forward to taking in these sights since before leaving their home. She loves the bustle of the waterfront and is utterly intrigued by the sight of the ships and men who visit the booming, southern port of Charles Towne. Anne has been reading stories about pirates and privateers who sail the length of the colonial seaboard raiding and plundering ships and then frequent the colonies harbors to exchange their booty for coins of the realm and to allow the rowdy and raucous crews to terrorize the shabby shacks and shanties where booze flows as freely as the women.

Stories of bold and audacious privateers have dominated both the newspapers and casual conversations of the day. She often thinks about the thrilling adventures, dangers, and freedom that would accompany such a wild and live-for-the-day existence. As she watches, her mind flits like the wind— whisking her away to imaginative thoughts of what a typical pirate voyage might be like. Her daydreaming is interrupted only when a man carelessly pushes a cart carefully balanced with a load of barrels directly into the path of their carriage.

Anne's body lunges forward as their carriage jerks to a sudden stop. They hear the loud yet dignified and muffled voice of their driver asserting to the hapless cooper, "You— yes you! Clear the path and do so promptly."

While the carriage sits idly waiting, Anne looks out the window and down the length of Front Street. How sensible, she considered for a moment, that the street that lines the harbor in every such town typically is called Front Street. As her mind draws in the many sights, she sees two men talking near the carriage—twenty or so feet away. One of the men, slender in stature, casts a quick and casual glance her way as the other continues to draw from his pipe and carry on the conversation.

For only a moment, Anne and the man lock eyes. Her years spent in the finest finishing schools tell her to look away, knowing that continuing to stare would not be ladylike. Anne's intrigued by the attention being directed toward her, she cannot stop her urge to look back at the rugged looking man.

The man smoking the pipe notices that his conversation has suddenly become a monologue instead of a dialog and that what he has been saying is falling on deaf ears. He stops talking and follows the direction of his friend's stare to see for himself what could possibly be more important than the thoughts of business he shares. He tracks the bearing of his friend's eyes to see them locked with a buxom young woman's in a passing carriage.

He laughs loudly, smacking his friend on the back, and says, "Well now, James Bonny, you act as though you've never laid eyes on such an angel before this day."

Anne faintly overhears James' reply, "Aye, mate; I do not believe I have not until this very moment."

The carriage lurches back into motion, and Anne leaves James with a seductive smile as they continue to the next corner and turn in the direction of their ultimate destination. James stands motionless, staring at the back of the carriage that carries away from him the most beautiful young lady he has, perhaps, ever seen.

He asks, to nobody in particular, and in a slow and deliberate voice, "Who might that be in the carriage?"

The pipe smoker steps up to stand beside James. "That would be the honorable William Cormac and his beautiful daughter, Anne. Word has it that she is as fiery and full of quest for life as she is lovely."

"Interesting," James utters slowly. "Very interesting."

CHAPTER FIVE

DISINHERITED

James Bonny is wildly attracted to Anne at first sight, but physical attraction isn't all that enters his mind as he thinks of Anne—the charming daughter of one of the city's wealthiest and most respected citizens. If he were simply looking to enjoy the pleasure of a woman's company, he knows that he has the choice of many women working at the brothels he frequents regularly.

James has a far grander plan in mind. Born into poverty, James has not enjoyed the benefits of a stable upbringing. Growing up on the streets of Charles Towne, he has learned that in order to survive, he has to fend for himself. At an early age he spends time near the waterfront, where he learns much from the inward and outward migration of deckhands and unsavory types who would spend their idle time—and money—in Charles Towne before shoving-off to their next port of call.

Bonny's word—the true mark of a man's character and worth in Colonial America—means little to either him or the many others with whom he has dealt over the years. As long as he sees a means to an end, he will lie, cheat and steal to get what he needs. If he plays his cards right, he is sure he can arrange for this spirited young flower of the South—Anne Cormac—to fall for and marry him. After which, of course, he will be able to lay claim to her inheritance—a fortune that will allow him to live the remainder of his life as a man of leisure. James begins to contemplate a plan of action. He does not realize that Anne has already conjured up a plan of her own.

James begins inquiring about William Cormac, learning as much as he can about him, including his place of business, the location of the Cormac estate, and which church the Cormac family attends. He disguises his inquiries by prefacing his many questions with the innocent-sounding charade that he is looking to gain employment at their estate as a stable keeper.

He learns that Cormac—like all families with roots in England—attends the large Anglican Church in Charles Towne. Better still, he discovers that young Anne attends every Sunday without fail. For weeks, James attends the services and strategically positions himself in the seats that are most visible to Anne. He also makes it a point to time both his arrivals and departures.

Within weeks, it's obvious to Anne that James is interested in her—their eyes have locked on numerous occasions and James once had the opportunity to bow graciously and allow her to exit from the pew to the central aisle before him. He used the opportunity to enjoy the view of her body from behind. Meanwhile, Anne has decided that James Bonny has a rough-hewn and edgy look that naturally fuels her interest in him—he comes with an element of danger that draws her in. He projects a sense of wild adventure and of pushing life to its limits. All of which suit Anne fine. Perfectly fine, actually.

Over the next few months, they begin meeting secretly and quickly become romantically involved. They are capable actors, and carry on with roles in the grand theater of life that are working perfectly—not knowing that both of their plans are designed to achieve the same short-term goal: marriage.

Their union ultimately will deliver different goals for each of them; James wants to marry Anne to gain access to her family's fortune, and Anne wants to marry James as a vehicle to find the adventure she longs for and gain independence from her domineering father. Being the keeper of the Cormac estate affords Anne the unrestricted ability to come and go as needed. This allows her to carry on her affair with James, and within a month, they are wed secretly.

After their short and simple ceremony, Anne and James step outside the chapel doors, Anne looks James up and down and says, "James, you area a handsome devil when polished up."

"Thank you, Mrs. Bonny, and may I inquire at which inn you fancy spending our wedding night?" Realizing that James is the most presentable she's ever seen him, Anne replies,

"The consummation of our vows will have to wait; we must first run one errand." James returns a quizzical look as Anne leads, climbing into her carriage without waiting for him to help her up, and having told the driver to "race like the wind" directly to the Cormac estate so that she may announce her new name to her father.

As the two enter the estate—husband and wife—to the astonishment of all, Anne grabs James' hand and pulls him to her father's parlor, where she knows he is likely spending this day as with most other days. She opens the heavy, stained oak doors to find her father seated at his desk sifting through stacks of documents. Anne steals her father's attention away; "Father," she inquires in a slightly playful voice. William raises his head and turns his attention from business to his daughter—strangely adorned in a full-length white dress.

He is surprised to see her with a young man who he has never seen before. Knowing that this man does not have his permission to call on Anne, he assumes that he is seeking employment at the estate.

"Annie, what might you need this fine evening?" Then he stands and addresses the stranger, saying, "And you, young sir, it's a bit late to gain an audience with me. I assume that you are looking for gainful employment." James and Anne cast a nervous and uncomfortably glance toward each other. At this moment, William instinctively senses that something is amiss. Something is quite different, he feels. He looks briefly at Anne and then addresses James again. "Employment?" James does not respond. While holding his hat, he looks nervously off to the side and coughs to clear his throat.

William then says, "Annie, what is the meaning of this? And you, sir, better find your tongue quickly before I lose my patience." Anne looks once again at James and then directs her attention to her father.

"Father, it's not employment that James seeks. He is here with me to announce that we have been wed."

For minutes on end, William Cormac's face is completely void of expression, as if his soul has been snatched from his body. He slowly stands and walks from behind his desk toward the parlor's fireplace. With his back turned to Anne and James, he leans against a brass stand that holds a collection of fireplace tools, as if to keep his body from collapsing. William repeats Anne's name several times before turning toward the couple and brandishing a large brass fireplace poker as though it were a sword.

Surprised, James takes a step backward and looks toward the room's doors—instinctively searching out his nearest exit for escape. In an out-of-control rage, William swings the poker and shatters a large crystal bowl to pieces. Shards from the exploding bowl fly throughout the room. "Annie, what have you done? And, you, you scoundrel! I would rather see you dead before me than let you continue this contemptuous charade. How dare you think for a moment that you can conspire behind my back and take my daughter's hand?"

"Father, it is I who have gone behind you and brought

this to be. I have found the soul I was meant to find, and it's not your decision whom I choose to love, marry and live out my life with."

William ponders for a minute, his blood pressure rising. He imagines for a moment that his daughter has broken all rules of high society and become pregnant—a thought he dismisses. "If you choose not to end this abomination of a relationship, I will disinherit you, Annie. You will no longer be my daughter and no longer my concern."

Cormac turns back to James, "And you, whatever your name is, you will not find your way into my home nor Anne's inheritance." Slowly setting the hot poker back in its stand next to the hearth, he calms himself ever so slightly and stares down to the floor as he continues his address to James. "See yourself out and do not return. If you do, you will learn that I am a gentleman, but also a wrathful man."

William looks up to see that his Annie is gone. She has used the moment to run up the broad stairway two steps at a time, flying into her room and almost upending her dressers and armoire in an effort to gather up some clothing.

Then Anne briskly walks to her father's bedroom, and steals money that she knows is hidden in his middle bureau drawer. She pauses—never has she stolen money from her father—or anyone else. She senses that all of that may change—and perhaps sooner rather than later. Anne vaults down the stairs, steps into the study just long enough to grab James by the forearm, and walks briskly to and then through the still-open front door.

Whistling for the two stallions she has saddled earlier in the day and left ready in the stables, she and James mount up and head down the long, magnolia-lined lane she had known for so many years. Together, they depart from the estate, Anne with an exhilarating sense of freedom and a sense of independence that she has been searching for since childhood. She does not look back.

James, however, does glance back to stare as the fine, large and beautiful estate grows smaller—watching as his prize quickly diminishes behind, and then finally disappears as the two steeds move through the first wide, arcing turn in the road that leads to Charles Towne at a healthy gallop.

He rides blank-faced, not yet fully comprehending why his plan has failed so miserably.

CHAPTER SIX

THE DEVIL'S DRINK

The sun has risen in New Providence on this summer day in 1717, and by midmorning, the day already promises to be hot and muggy. Inside a rickety but otherwise comfortable wooden inn on Bay Street, Jack Rackham awakens to the morning sun shining through burlap curtains and the sound of screeching seagulls diving for small fry on the bay. His head is foggy from an evening of libations that had lasted far too long, and his mouth still has the distinct taste of rum.

The breezeless room is already growing hot, and Jack throws aside the light linen that partially covers his naked body. He looks next to him to see a woman, also naked, sleeping soundly on her stomach with her face buried in her pillow. He can only assume that he left the tavern with one of the many ladies of the night who frequent the place. These opportunistic women know that there's no shortage of money spent by the many traveling men who pass through the bustling port, coming and going to do whatever business they do, looking for a good time.

The sound of men outside the room's open window this early in the day captures his curiosity. The words increase in volume and speed and Jack surmises that some issue or other is at hand. In addition, he knows that issues usually mean opportunity. As he dresses, he sits hard on the edge of the bed to put on his boots and awakens his companion. The sun is now streaking across the side of her face causing her to clinch her eyes shut. "Jack, you randy dog, are you leaving me?" she asks.

"Aye, lass, I have to see what all the fuss is about near the docks." She raises her head slightly to listen for a moment before gently settling back down and using the pillow to cover her ears. "But lying with your backside to me and with your face buried in that pillow, I can't tell to whom I paid a king's ransom for the passion I can barely recollect ... too much drink. Which lass might you be? Mary? No, Mary has a broader arse ... maybe Elizabeth?"

The woman rolls over to reveal her identity. "Ahhh, Nancy, the princess of New Providence. A very good morning to you," he says as he reaches across to deliver a smack upon the woman's backside. As Jack begins buttoning his shirt, he continues, "Lass, as red wine is the drink of Christ, rum is truly the devil's drink. And you, my dear, are a curious blend of both."

Nancy props herself up on her elbows, allowing the sheet to fall back to reveal her large and creamy white breast and looks at Jack with a coy smile. "Well, Captain Rackham, with that kind-a talk, you've just bought yourself another go at it."

"Nancy, the Lord has truly blessed ye with a profound talent," Jack says as he fastens—and just as quickly begins to undo—the top button of his loose-fitting white blouse. "Woman, with that proposition, I am happy to oblige you. The world will have to wait a fathom or two to see Jack Rackham this day."

CHAPTER SEVEN

THE PRIVATEER

Seven years earlier.

A middle-aged man wearing a heavy night robe sits at a modest wooden desk set in a large dank room devoid of both décor and color. It is midafternoon and outside, the day is bright—sunlight pours through the room's large-paned window. The man uses his thumb and index finger to playfully twirl a quill pen sporting a brownish-gray plume. He dabs his pen into the small, square glass inkwell to replenish the fuel needed to continue the flow of words from his mind onto paper.

The man tilts his head slightly to one side and looks off into oblivion as he ponders the perfect wording for his next line of thought. He takes a deep breath, places his pen down on the table, stands from his chair, and stretches both arms high into the air. He takes off his robe and lies down in his bed, falling quickly into a deep sleep. He begins to dream almost immediately—his eyes flitting back and forth behind their lids.

A sudden bright flash occurs, revealing ... a man yelling as loudly as he can. Wind, rain and powerful waves driven by a tropical storm bear down on him and slosh down the deck and out the scuppers of the ship's deck on which he stands. The noise of the wind whistling through the ship's rigging drowns out his attempts to communicate to the other men holding fast to any available rigging or railing at hand to keep from being swept overboard and into the raging sea. A large wave crashes down directly atop of the man knocking him from his feet. As he emerges from the wave, he whips his head backward, flinging his long mop of hair away from his face. *"We must save the Duchess!"* he yells with all the strength, volume and motivation he can muster.

A sudden bright flash occurs, revealing ... a sun-filled day aboard the deck of a large frigate that sails swiftly away from a small isle in the Pacific Ocean. A tall man with sharp features uses a telescopic brass spyglass to observe smoke billowing from a fire on a nearby beach. He sees a man frantically jumping up and down and flailing his arms in the air in an attempt to gain the attention of his passing ship. With a slight chuckle, the seaman hands his spyglass to a younger man standing by his side. He looks through the spyglass and the two begin laughing at the sight of the frantic man on the shore. *A sudden bright flash occurs, shifting time forward, revealing* ... the man from the beach now aboard the ship and below deck, sitting at a table as a plate of food is placed before him. Ignoring eating utensils, he frantically shovels food into his mouth with his hands. The dirt-crusted man with his three-foot long dark brown beard wears primitively stitched together goatskins for clothing. In a hollowed voice he says, "Aye, been marooned on that patch of God forsaken land for nearly five years."

A sudden bright flash occurs, revealing … chaos of a brutal battle taking place aboard a ship's deck. Grenade explosions ring out, followed by the sounds of muskets firing. Metal cutlasses chatter as they collide, their sounds mixed with grunting, yelling, and the unmistakable painful cries of men becoming casualties. *A sudden bright flash occurs, shifting time forward, revealing* … a musket ball striking a young man's body. The projectile fractures two ribs. As he releases a painful yell, a saber is thrust toward his body. The blade penetrates his lower back and swiftly glides through his torso. The razor-sharp blade slices through the man's stomach and intestines. He feels pressure, but no pain as he looks down, to see a foot-and-a-half-long blood-coated steel blade emerging from his abdomen. From the background, a man's voice is heard yelling, "Noooo!" *A sudden bright flash occurs, shifting time forward, revealing* … a man sitting on a smoky, bloodstained deck cradling a younger man's lifeless body. He looks into the dead man's open but empty eyes and rocks in a back-and-forth motion. The man's breathing is labored because he is bleeding heavily from his mouth. During the battle, he was shot in the face. A musket ball slammed into his jawbone and instantly shattered it. The impact of the musket ball against bone caused the projectile to fracture. The largest pieces of lead ripped through his cheek and embedded in the roof of his mouth. As he tries to speak, the increasing flow of blood pools in his mouth and pours down his throat coating his vocal chords and impairing his ability to speak. He manages to enunciate one garbled word, "Brother."

Woodes Rogers suddenly wakes and gasps for air. In one fluid motion, he throws aside the quilt that covers him, rolls over, and sits up on the edge of his bed. He turns his head side-to-side and rolls his shoulders in an effort to relax his tensed muscles. Then, in frustration, he rubs his face with his hands and stands. Rogers has been waking up night after night from the same dream for months, his clothes dampened with sweat. The dream haunts him deeply and chronicles several events that took place during one of his long privateer expeditions. The expedition had begun with such high hopes of success. The outcome that everyone expected was to take enough treasure and goods from Spanish shipping to return a healthy profit to the expedition's investors and make enough money for him and his crew to live comfortably for the rest of their lives. For Rogers, the stakes were higher than for most of the men sailing with him. His past business dealings had put his family in dire straits, and if this expedition did not yield a good profit, he would not have enough money to pay off their debts. He and his family would be bankrupt.

Rogers recalls how full of optimism he was before he embarked on his expedition. He remembers the excitement he felt when he raised the money needed to fund the voyage and received a Letter of Marquee from the English government that legalized their intent to attack Spanish shipping. The expedition's 256 shares were issued to a group of Bristol businessmen. These shares were taken up by a relatively small group of merchants, including many prominent Bristolians such as mayors, ex-mayors, sheriffs, aldermen, town clerks, and physicians. The person who bought the most shares and became the principal investor in the voyage was Thomas Goldney II, a Bristol grocer who had purchased 36 shares.

In his excitement to set sail, Rogers quickly planned his expedition and assembled his crew consisting of 183 men aboard his 30-gun, 320-ton frigate the *Duke* and 150 men aboard his second 260-ton ship the *Duchess*. He recalls that all hopes and spirits were high as he sailed his ships from the Port of Bristol on the first day of August 1708. When Rogers' ships finally returned from their expedition, dropping anchor in London on the Thames River on the fourteenth day of October 1711, Rogers, his ships, and their crews were battered and scarred. Over three years at sea, taking the fight to the Spanish and battling harsh weather conditions changed everyone. The carnage Rogers witnessed and the damage he inflicted upon others progressively chipped away at his soul. The pain of seeing his younger brother mortally wounded and die in his arms ruined his spirit. He returned a broken man.

Rogers has been away from home for nearly a year when Sarah begins to worry that their young children might not remember their father and takes on the responsibility to keep his memory alive. Three nights a week, when they sit down for dinner, they join hands for prayer and while they eat, she tells them stories about him. The children listen intently to stories about his childhood, about his sea adventures as a younger man and about experiences during his current expedition that she selects from the letters he sends to her while anchored in exotic ports.

The letters she receives from Woodes during the first year project a tone of excitement and enthusiasm. Two years into his expedition, Woodes seems disenchanted and begins questioning basic human values. A segment of one letter she receives stands out from the others and concerns her.

Woodes writes, *"Dearest Sarah, after capturing a vessel near the coast of Brazil, we anchored in a calm lagoon. Along with this ship, we also took on a number of prisoners. Our plans were to take our captives off the ship while we searched and relieved it of its valuables. We then planned to release our captives that evening before continuing on our southern course following the Brazilian coastline.*

Late that afternoon, while on shore, I heard the sound of what I presumed to be a wounded animal in the distance. I grabbed my musket and followed the sound into the jungle. As I ventured deeper into the jungle, the sounds of the suffering animal became louder but I still had no clue of the type of animal I would eventually encounter. I soon came upon a clearing, and through the trees and heavy vegetation, I could see movement. As I drew closer, I quietly hid myself behind a large fallen tree. I could not believe my eyes. I spied a half-clothed man covered completely in blood. I then noticed another man, also covered in blood, standing completely naked against a tree and making guttural sounds. It was late afternoon and the sun was lowering. The dense jungle canopy was allowing only a miniscule amount of sunlight to pass through to the jungle's floor. My vision was hindered, so I moved even closer to gain a better vantage point. I soon noticed that the man closest to me was wielding a knife, and the man standing against the tree was actually tied to it and being skinned alive. When I realized what was taking place, I yelled at the man holding the knife, ordering him to stop what he was doing and stand down. The surprised man turned toward me and revealed his identity. It was Matthew Smith, one of the cooks sailing aboard my ship. I will never forget the look of insanity he gave me and how the whites of his eyes stood out against his pure red, blood-soaked face. We were momentarily frozen in time, as we both stood staring at each other. The skinned man began moving his restrained body violently, trying to free himself from the ropes that bound him tightly against the tree. I yelled, "Matthew!" He quickly turned, thrust his knife into the chest of the restrained man, and began running into the jungle. I pursued him, and when he would not obey my orders to stop, I put him down with musket fire.

After witnessing this horrific act of cruelty and the insanity that men are capable of during times of battle, I am beginning to question if man is born inherently good as our church has taught us. If man is born of innocence, does evil enter the body after living in a world of sin and corruption? Or, is evil within the soul from conception, sharing space and coexisting with good? Do good souls succumb to evil? I have seen more evil on this expedition than I care to speak of. I cannot explain what caused Matthew Smith to do what he did.

I speculate that when our prisoners were brought to shore, Smith forced the man into the jungle, threatening him with a pistol. How other crewmembers did not see this take place I will never know. Many of us believe that his act was premeditated. Smith planned his actions and knew what he wanted to do with his captive. At some point, Smith must have knocked the man unconscious and tied him to the tree. He then began carving on the poor soul."

Your ever devoted,

Woodes

Rogers does not include what happened next, when writing his letter. After shooting Matthew Smith in the jungle, Rogers returns to the clearing. He looks closely at the dead man still tied to the tree with only the handle of Smith's knife protruding from his chest. The only remaining skin left on the man is located on his left forearm to his fingers. The man is unrecognizable, but Rogers believes that he is one of the men they took as a prisoner earlier that day. He notices that both eyeballs and ears have been removed. He also learns why the man made such strange noises and could not speak. His tongue was cut from his mouth. Rogers notices that other pieces of the man's body have been removed, including eight of his toes and most of his fingers on his right hand. Rogers investigates the area and sees a cooking pot positioned over a small open fire. He walks over to the pot, lifts the lid, and looks in to see the man's eyeballs and tongue boiling with carrots and potatoes.

The victim's fingers, ears, toes, and skin were neatly placed next to the pot on a wooden cutting board alongside a butcher's knife. Rogers covers his mouth, feeling that he is going to vomit. He says to himself, *My God, he was cooking and eating the poor devil alive!* Rogers returns to his ship and sends his men into the jungle to gather the two bodies.

After three years, his letters become infrequent and when his wife does receive the letters, they take on a darker tone. The last letter she receives delivers tragic news.

Woodes writes, *My Dearest Sarah, I am saddened to inform you that my brother Jonathan was killed during a fierce battle against the Spanish. As I realized he was close to death, I prayed with all my being for God not to take him from us. Only minutes later, he died in my arms on the deck of the Spanish vessel he helped capture. I cursed God the day I buried him, along with thirty-two other crewmembers, beneath a row of palm trees on a small island in the Pacific Ocean. I no longer have the desire, nor the ambition, to carry on with our expedition. I have ordered my ships to begin our journey back to England.*

Your ever devoted,

Woodes

As Sarah finishes reading the letter, her eyes overflow with tears.

Chapter Eight

Seclusion

Not long after Woodes returns home to his family, Sarah realizes that he's a decidedly different person from the passionately optimistic man she knew before he left. He wakes almost every night thrashing from his dreams, and when she tries talking to him about what continues to torment him, he does not confide in her. Sarah also notices something that disturbs her. When she looks deep into her husband's eyes, she sees an emptiness that gives her an uneasy feeling. It's as though he no longer knows how to respond to her affection or how to provide the attention that his two daughters and son long for. Sarah decides that her husband needs time to readjust to life in Bristol after being at sea for so long.

No matter how hard she tries, their situation worsens. Woodes cannot resurrect the feelings he once had for his wife and children. After being home for only two weeks, he realizes that living under the same roof is impossible and makes the decision to leave his family.

As he prepares to leave, he tells Sarah, "I cannot explain why it is best that I leave because I do not know myself. I no longer feel emotion the way I did before my expedition. I am empty and void of feelings. I am beginning to fear that our marriage and the balance of my life will become unfortunate casualties of my condition." As he walks out the door, he stops and turns to face Sarah. "As I find my way, I will forward what I can to help support our children." He hands her an envelope with its string clasp securely fastened. "This is most of my remaining value. It is not much, but it will provide you and the children essentials for several months. I suggest that you all take refuge by living at your parents' estate. I have no doubt that they will welcome you with open arms."

Woodes and Sarah both know that if they ever needed to turn to her family for support, it would be given without hesitation. Sarah is the daughter of Rear Admiral Sir William Whetstone. The Whetstone family is one of the most the prominent families in Bristol.

Rogers removes himself from society and goes into seclusion. He rents a single large room in the lower rent district of London. His second story room faces south and overlooks a narrow cobblestone street only three blocks from the Thames River. As he closes the door to his room, Rogers notices two wooden crates placed against the wall. He realizes that these crates hold two cases of gin that he arranged to be delivered earlier that day. He wedges open the fastened top of the highest stacked crate. The force placed upon the wooden top causes it to release a loud groan and a sharp snap from the friction against the wood and nails being pulled apart. Rogers tosses the top off to the side and lifts one of the bottles from the hay-lined box. He turns toward the sunlight shining through the room's window, raises the bottle in front of his face, looks through the container holding the colorless alcohol and says, "It is good to see you again old friend." Rogers immerses himself in an alcoholic binge that lasts for two weeks. As he passes in and out of consciousness, he ends up in an alcohol-induced coma, lying prostrate across his large bed. While he sleeps, he begins having his recurring dream that ends with his brother Jonathan dying in his arms. As he looks into his brother's lifeless eyes and says, "Brother," his brain fires off electrical impulses to his nerve endings that deliver the cue for his body to wake from the dream as it always does. His muscles contract and he wakes in a cold sweat, gasping for air.

Still inebriated and barely able to function, Rogers reaches for the pistol he placed on the nightstand beside his bed. As he grabs the loaded gun, he knocks two emptied gin bottles onto the floor, sits up on the edge of his bed and begins to cry. He places the end of the pistol barrel under his chin and moves his index finger onto the pistol's trigger as he readies himself for death. A second from squeezing the trigger, he looks straight ahead and is startled by the sight of a man staring directly at him from across the room. Rogers yells, "Who are you?" How did you enter my room?" His impaired mind takes a moment to process and make sense of what's happening. He realizes that the staring intruder is only a reflection of himself in a large floor mirror set across the room. Although it's the middle of the night, he can see his image due to the light being cast from a full moon. He looks at his reflection and the pistol snugly positioned under his chin and yells angrily. He quickly removes the pistol's barrel, takes aim at his reflection and pulls the trigger. In an instant, the gunpowder ignites and illuminates the room as the loud explosion sounds. The mirror shatters, sending thousands of glass shards flying in the opposite direction of the gunfire. Rogers drops his pistol to the floor. His body becomes limp as he slowly slides from the edge of the bed and down to a sitting position on the floor. With his back against his bed, he cries himself to sleep.

At eleven o'clock the next morning, the sunlight and the faint sound of two people arguing in the hallway outside his room waken him. The bright sunlight irritates his dehydrated and bloodshot eyes. He looks around his room and sees emptied gin bottles, half-eaten meals, scattered papers, and dried patches of vomit. His eyes continue scanning the room as he pauses at the sight of a large floor mirror frame void of its mirror. He looks at the pieces of glass on the floor and notices a bullet hole in the wall. His eyes continue to follow the contour of the wall until settling on the stack of forty-two journals that he used to document daily events while at sea. After weeks of self-inflicted torture, he realizes that the gallons of gin he's consumed and solitude are only making matters worse for him.

Rogers picks up a journal and begins reading. He considers that reading the journals from beginning to end could help him sort through his thoughts and might help cleanse his soul. As he reads, he begins writing notes, adding details he now remembers but did not document at the time of his voyages. He begins to use what he reads and the additional details from his memory as material for writing a book that chronicles his experiences. He sets out from his room months later with a completed manuscript for a book he titles "*A Cruising Voyage Round the World.*"

When he emerges from his solitude, he finds himself engaged in a different type of battle. During the time he sailed his ships back to England, Rogers desperately needed medical treatment for the wounds he suffered while battling the Spanish. His ships set a course for the neutral Dutch port of Batavia, in what is now Indonesia, where Rogers underwent surgery to remove the fragments of the musket ball still embedded in the roof of his mouth. The operation was successful, but the swelling caused by the surgery leaves Rogers unable to speak for days. While recovering, he continues to issue orders using pen and paper. Rogers orders his quartermaster to replenish their supplies and to inspect the seaworthiness of the *Duke* and *Duchess* and the two ships they captured. After the inspection, it was determined that one of two ships they have captured was not in the condition needed to survive the long voyage back to England. With this news, Rogers orders his first mate to seek a buyer and sell the vessel for scrap before leaving port. The ship was sold to the Dutch. By dealing with the Dutch, Rogers unknowingly committed a violation of the British East India Company's monopoly. Upon his return, a legal dispute ensued between the expedition investors and the British East India Company. As settlement for their claim for breach of monopoly, the investors paid the British East India Company a sizable percentage of the total value that Rogers brought back from his expedition. Although Rogers doubled the money that the investors originally used to fund the expedition, he only managed to gain a modest amount of money from a voyage that took years from his life, left him disfigured, and cost the life of his younger brother. The money he made from the expedition was less than he could have made at home and was entirely absorbed by the debts his family had incurred in his absence. After failing to recoup his losses from the expedition, Rogers was forced to sell his family home in Bristol. He was also successfully sued by a group of over 200 of his former crewmembers asserting that they had not received their fair share of the expedition's profits. The profits from his book were not enough to overcome these setbacks, and he was forced into bankruptcy. Now in complete financial ruin, Woodes and Sarah became permanently separated.

On his own and with very little money, Rogers realizes that the only thing in his favor is that tales from his expedition and his book have brought him notoriety. All of England celebrates Rogers as a national hero for being the first Englishman to circumnavigate the globe, and having returned with his original ships and most of his original crew. The account of his victory over the Spanish warship *Nuestra Señora de la Incarnación Disenganio* has added to the fervor. His meteoric rise to celebrity status is the only remaining thing in his life that he can recognize as being positive, but fame without fortune does not satisfy Rogers. He uses his notoriety while it can still benefit him and believes that the only direction out of his financial difficulty is to lead another expedition and sets sail in the spring of 1713.

This time, Rogers approaches the East India Company to fund his expedition, and they agree to have Rogers purchase slaves on the Eastern African island of Madagascar and transport them to the Dutch East Indies for auction. Rogers has a secondary purpose to accomplish during his Madagascar expedition. He plans to assess the viability of establishing a British colony on the island. It is common knowledge that pirates use Madagascar for their base of operations. To colonize Madagascar, the pirates must be either vanquished or reformed. To Rogers' surprise, when collecting information on pirate activities, he finds that a large number of the pirates have already begun to colonize the island. Although basic, Rogers realizes that the makeshift pirate town might serve as the cornerstone of the formation of a true colony in the future. During his time on the island, while purchasing slaves and preparing the human cargo for transport, he can persuade many of the local island pirates to sign a petition to Queen Anne asking her for clemency.

Even though Rogers' expedition is profitable, when he returns to London in 1715, the East India Company vetoes Rogers' proposed colonial expedition to Madagascar. They believe that investing in organizing a colony initially populated with pirates is a greater threat to its monopoly than allowing the pirates to continue as an unorganized group. Accordingly, Rogers turns his sights from Madagascar to the West Indies.

CHAPTER NINE

A KINGS COMMISSION

After Britain's Queen Anne dies in midsummer of 1714, her husband George ascends to the throne and becomes king. Several of Rogers' friends receive appointments to advise the newly crowned king. He asks these friends to become his conduit to the king, putting forth his name any time possible opportunities present themselves. Surely enough, the name "Captain Woodes Rogers" comes up numerous times as the king considers candidates to appoint by commission to a number of vacant posts.

King George devotes the first three years of his reign to familiarizing himself with all matters of state, including the best strategies for advancing the British Empire's plans for expansion while limiting the expansion of the empire's principal rivals, Spain and France.

In early 1717, Rogers—to his pleasant surprise—receives a summons from King George to meet at Windsor Castle. He travels by horse-drawn carriage through the English countryside to the county of Berkshire. Halfway through his journey, Rogers uses the blunt brass handle of his walking cane to knock on the cabin's interior ceiling directly underneath the coachman's seat. The noise gets the attention of the driver who gently pulls back on the reins of the two rusty-brown, muscular quarter horses and brings the carriage to a stop. The coachman ties off the horses' reins and leans over to the side of the coach. "Did you knock guv-nah?"

Leaning over and speaking upward through the carriage window, he replies, "Indeed. Could you please inform me when the castle comes into view?"

"Aye captain, that I will do." Taking the reins back into his gloved hands, the coachman gives them a brisk whiplike jostle and urges the horses forward with an encouraging, but authoritative, "Let's move along now."

Forty minutes later, the carriage bounces roughly and then leans, first to one side and then the other as the driver guides the wheels through a rough patch of road. Through the hollowed clatter of the horses' hooves and vibrations of the carriage, Rogers hears the voice of the coachman. "Guv-nah, we are approaching Eaton. Windsor Castle is in the distance."

As the carriage maneuvers on the narrow road that slowly curves through the small country village at the foot of the castle mount, Rogers hears children playing and leaning forward to cast a glance through the curtained window. He sees that the carriage is passing The King's College of Our Lady of Eton, a well-known and respected school for boys.

He sticks his head far enough outside the carriage window to see the castle sitting majestically—high up and directly in front of him. He marvels at the sight of the enormous edifice that surrounds the castle, how it dominates the landscape and looms over Eaton like a father keeping protective watch over a small child.

The thought that the original foundations of the castle dated back more than seven hundred years to the reign of William the Conqueror fascinates him. As the carriage draws closer, he imagines how the king's knights must have looked as they rode to and fro through the castle's massive gates wearing heavy shells of armor. Continuing on down the castle's quarter-mile-long ash road, lined on both sides by a column of large black oaks, the carriage soon pulls up to the structure's heavily guarded main entrance. England is at war, and the castle is heavily garrisoned, manned by more than a thousand of England's finest soldiers—a full regiment—along with hundreds of traditional camp followers—a combination of servants, cooks, stablemen, blacksmiths, and more than a handful of ladies of pleasure, all to support the elite troops responsible for protecting the king and seeing to his every need and comfort.

Five hundred additional troops camp near the castle, providing added support and ensuring the king's safety whenever he is in residence at Windsor. The coach carrying Rogers enters the castle, and both he and the driver dismount as several livery boys take the reins and lead the horses off toward the stables at the rear of the massive stone structure.

Within a few minutes, Rogers is following an escort through a labyrinthine maze of halls, rooms, and courtyards to one of the castle's many libraries.

One of the king's servants appears and in a firm and solid military voice bellows to Rogers, "His Majesty will join you soon. Please make yourself comfortable." Rogers acknowledges the servant with a simple, "Thank you." The servant delivers a quick bow as he leaves through one of the impressive room's many doors. Rogers takes a quick glance around, deciding to himself that there must be many thousands of books in the massive room, which contains two balconies at varying levels. Several beautifully carved wooden ladders on rollers provide access to the highest shelves, perhaps reaching forty feet or more.

Six large oak tables, each probably weighing a half-ton, sit on the cold gray slate floor. An enormous open-sided stone fireplace dominates the center of the room, its flue extending straight upward through the ceiling and a pleasant fire brings warmth while also drawing away the dampness in the air. Rogers clasps his hands behind his back as he paces in front of the bookcases, making note of some of the more interesting book titles. He easily spots William Shakespeare's *Hamlet* and *Macbeth*. As he continues looking, he spots other titles that interest him, including *The Works of Leonardo di ser Piero da Vinci* and *The Travels of Marco Polo*.

A loud snap, sparked from one log falling through another amid the warm coals of the fireplace, takes his attention away from the bookcases. Turning his head toward the noise, he spots two books laid out on top of the table nearest the fire. Curiosity gets the best of him as he walks over to the table and reads the title from the cover of the book closest to him, Sun Tzu's *The Art of War*. The other book lies open, hiding its front cover and title. As Rogers edges closer to read the text on the dimly lit pages, he recognizes the words he's reading as unmistakably his own. The silence is suddenly broken by a voice from the doorway.

"One of the most interesting books ever conceived, Sun Tzu's *The Art of War*, written in the 6th century BC." Rogers turns to find King George standing at the room's main entrance. The king continues, "I am told by one of my top generals that the brilliance of Sun Tzu's strategies lies in their simplicity. Strategists will likely study his tactics for a thousand years to come. I've read it many times myself. If you have not yet read it, Captain Rogers, I would urge you to do so. You will recognize the other most recent book I have read—it is a most fascinating story of courage, overcoming adversity and achieving ultimate success. You know it well." The king reaches out and picks up the book, running the fingers of one hand up and down the smooth leather cover. A *Cruising Voyage Round the World*.

"Captain Rogers, welcome to Windsor."

"Your Majesty, I consider it a great pleasure for me to be your guest this day, and I am honored that you have taken an interest in my humble story."

King George responds, "Your expeditions and book have made you very popular among the English people. I, myself, read your book after my closest advisor gave me an edition and insisted that I do so. I found your stories both entertaining and educational. I was told that you dedicated a full third of your book to describing in meticulous detail all of the many distant lands you visited during your adventures, with the intent of providing future expeditions with the insights they would need to increase their odds of completing successful voyages. I found this an admirable gesture."

The king continued, "I was greatly fascinated, in particular, with the story of your rescue of the marooned gentleman, Selkirk. I cannot imagine surviving all alone on a small island in the Pacific for close to five years. I must also tell you that I was deeply moved by the loss of your brother during your glorious battle against the Spanish.

"Since assuming the throne, I have spent the vast majority of my time learning everything I can about the dealings of the empire and the decisions I must make to ensure that it remains strong and continues to prosper. As it stands today, the balance of power among the European kingdoms remains unstable. Stability will come and go as time passes, just as countries inevitably will continue to find reasons to wage war. In this age of adventure, England continually looks to conquer and influence new territories throughout the world. I envision an empire upon which the sun never sets—that is my dream and my goal.

"I would guess that this race for supremacy will continue until there is no longer land to claim. When considering the expansion of our empire, I look to both our east and west to ascertain which possesses the greatest opportunities—which regions will provide the greatest reward for the smallest investment in both time and treasure.

When looking to the east, I see bountiful natural resources that will add immensely to our wealth; however, the terrain and the many cultures are diverse, and the people who inhabit these lands could be difficult to assimilate. When looking to the west, I see our colonies across the Atlantic flourishing. I am told that the resources farther to the west of our colonies there are vast and incalculable. The natives are said to be primitive, and I have been led to believe they might be easily conquered. Yes, captain, I believe that the west is important to the future expansion of our empire.

"Although we have established a strong foothold in the Americas with our colonial presence, there is a great race currently taking place. The Spanish and French are encroaching on our colonies, the Spanish from the south and the French from the north and west."

Rogers nods his head, assuring the king that he has his full attention.

"Captain Rogers. All races have a beginning, middle and an end. Races can be won or lost at any given time and for any of a hundred or more unforeseen reasons. The master of the western hemisphere has yet to be determined. Do you understand my meaning?"

"Yes, Your Highness, I do understand. The Spanish control the south and the French have established a significant presence in the north and also within the still-unexplored territories west of our colonies. They have navigated from the headwaters of the great river that divides the land all the way to the Gulf west of Florida. For England to continue to prosper in America, we must control this land. Not some of it, but all of it." Rogers delivers the summation he knows the king expects "Your Highness, it is imperative that we remove the Spanish and French from the continent."

"Captain, I have long waited for the opportunity to talk with you in person, to better understand the type of man you are. I am considering you for a commission that would give you the command of a territory that is believed to hold great strategic value for the Crown. You would, in effect, be my representative—my regent—with all the powers and authority such a position would entail." Rogers stiffened himself, expecting the next words to come. The king spoke, "If England was to call upon you to serve as I have thus described, would you serve her loyally?"

"Yes, Your Highness, It would be my honor to serve England—and, equally important—promise a life of honor and fidelity to the king who rules her."

Pausing to reflect, Rogers realizes that the last expedition paid him well, and he has been waiting years for his popularity to repay him fully for all of his sacrifice. His influential friends, advisors to the king, have judiciously lobbied on Rogers' behalf consistently for nearly three years. Receiving a commission directly from His Majesty would be a tremendous honor that could lead to living out the remainder of his life as a wealthy man. He allows himself to savor the moment.

King George smiles in response to Rogers' answer. "After reading your book, learning more about you and meeting you in the flesh, I have determined that you possess the combination of skills making you well-suited to undertake the commission I describe and to command the region—a region including the islands of the Bahamas and much of the tremendously profitable West Indies along the eastern edge of the Caribbean." Turning to face Captain Rogers, the king asks, "Are you familiar with this region of the world?"

"Yes, your Highness, indeed I am. The fact that the region is comprised of more than 700 islands, islets, reefs and cays fascinate me. After finishing my last expedition, I thought I would turn my attention toward the West Indies. I find it amusing that the islands were named the West Indies due to an incredible navigational error. Imagine Columbus' embarrassment had he ever learned he landed his ships upon the shores of a new continent rather than the Asian islands he intended to reach. I am sure the expression on his face would have been priceless," Rogers offered with a grin.

"Indeed, I am sure Columbus could never have imagined the future importance of the discovery he made. The riches drawn from the Indies have defined the order of world power for two centuries. It is now our turn to command the region. I have recently appointed Sir Nicolas Lawes to assume the duties of the Royal Governor of Jamaica. I expect you and Sir Lawes will work well together to plan and coordinate your efforts."

The more the king speaks, the more attentive Rogers becomes.

Continuing on, the king looks directly at his captain-turned-viceroy saying, "I've corresponded with the governor of Bermuda, learning the Spanish abandoned their post years ago after a devastating hurricane. Since then, the Bahamas have had no face or form of government. The region has become a rogue's gallery of infamous rascals—all enemies of the Crown. An absent landlord currently governs these islands. He has done nothing to deter the wicked work of these pirates and privateers who answer only to themselves.

Under the terms of your commission, the current landlord agrees to lease the rights of the islands for a token sum, to a company that will fall under your control. The lease will be in place for a period of twenty-one years. In exchange for ridding the islands of pirate activities, restoring trade, and defending the islands as a British colony, a healthy share of the colony's profits will be yours."

"Your Highness, you are very generous."

"Captain, I believe your experience as a skilled navigator, sea commander, and privateer will be the assets we need to secure order in this region."

"I have become quite familiar with the tremendous natural beauty of those islands and seas, my Lord. I've learned they are as rugged and risky as they are beautiful." The king nods. Rogers continues, "Many of the islands are infested with unsavory sorts—both primitive natives and European buccaneers. And I understand that a number of pirate captains use New Providence as their base of operations."

"I believe it would benefit us greatly if you were to convert the more proficient of these pirates to privateers working in the service of England—working for you. If these scoundrels can be allied with us through clemency and Letters of Marquee, they could completely disrupt Spanish and French trade from sailing in Caribbean waters for years. They would extend our power there and pay their own way in the process." A broad grin crossed the king's face.

Rogers responds, "Your Highness, I have always considered it ingenious in times of war for governments to legalize piracy for the benefit of attacking their enemies' vessels. Privateering is an effective way for a navy to recruit mercenaries and their ships for little or no expense. Roving the seas as a privateer for a good portion of my life, I understand well how a pirate thinks. If propositioned correctly, the more intelligent ones will quickly realize that they can continue their activities under the protection of a Letter of Marquee and with fewer targets to attack.

"The ones that we cannot convert will be the idealistic variety. These men choose piracy for more than the opportunity to sack ships. They typically attract more dangerous crews. They believe in piracy and all that it stands for—an independent society and all that entails," Rogers took his turn to scan the lofty shelves and share his thoughts—the benefits of his experiences at sea.

"I believe that half or more of the pirates based out of, say, New Providence will accept the pardon we extend. The rest will either relocate or disappear altogether. The few trying to remain and conduct business will be tracked down and arrested." Looking squarely at the king, Rogers pronounced the verdict, "I will hunt them down and kill them—to the last." The king nods in approval as Rogers continues, "My Lord, I will have the area cleared of the scourge of filthy pirates in twelve to twenty-four months."

The king pauses briefly and says, "Whenever I talk of pirates, I am visited by a childhood memory. When a young man growing up in Hanover, I entered military school and studied the history of the Roman Empire and its many emperors. One of my lessons involved a story that has remained etched in my mind. The event took place during the first century BC, when pirate states along the Anatolian coast threatened the commerce of the Roman Empire in the eastern Mediterranean.

"On a voyage across the Aegean Sea, Julius Caesar was kidnapped by Sicilian pirates and held prisoner on the Dodecanese islet of Pharmacusa. He maintained an attitude of superiority and good cheer throughout captivity. When the pirates told Caesar of their plans to demand a ransom of twenty talents of gold, Caesar was said to have laughed, insisting he was worth at least fifty. The pirates listened and raised their ransom. After Rome paid the ransom, Caesar was released. Upon his release, Caesar raised a fleet and captured the pirates and recovered a good portion of his own ransom.

"Caesar took the prisoners to a place near the village where they held him captive. He ordered his soldiers to erect a prison camp just outside the village walls. Next, he built anticipation as to what was to come in the minds of the prisoners and the villagers. He felt giving them all time to anticipate the inevitable would have a far greater impact than if he were simply to kill the prisoners quickly and sail back to Rome.

Rogers moved over to enjoy the warmth of the late afternoon sun and looked back at his host, enjoying the story. The king continued. "Caesar spent a number of days deciding which method to use in ending the lives of the prisoners. A week passed. Then the mighty Caesar announced that the prisoners' execution was to take place two days later.

The day before the planned execution, he had the prisoners bound together and paraded through the streets of the village. Several centurions invited the villagers to join the great Caesar in celebrating the death of Rome's enemies."

"On the day of the execution, each of the 120 prisoners was ordered into a single file line and told to drop to their knees. As they knelt, their feet and legs were quickly strapped to the ground. Long wooden rails were suspended and secured atop posts three and half feet from the ground on both the right and left sides of the men. The prisoners were ordered to place their arms over the wooden rails. Their arms were then pulled behind their backs and their wrists bound with tethers. This would keep them on their knees, preventing their bodies from falling to the ground.

"Each man was then fitted with a necklace of long thorns so that they could not bow or turn their heads, and each man's eyes were prevented from closing by simply using small twigs that were wedged against the tops of their cheekbones, pinning their eyelids open against their brow bones. Caesar wanted to ensure that they would see all that was about to take place.

"This simple but meticulous display was carried out so that each prisoner could not avoid the sight of each of his comrades being put to death before him. The line began with the lowest ranks and ended with the highest-ranking pirate commanders. The first man to be executed was the luckiest to die that day. He only saw the villagers' faces wince at the moment that the Praetorian's broad, sharp sword struck the back of his neck. The other captives could only wait and watch as each man's head was severed from his body.

"When all the heads were removed, Caesar had his men break camp and sail back to Rome. He left the bodies of his former captors untouched and bound to the wooden rails, each man's head displayed on the end of a long wooden pike by his side.

"The execution of the 120 prisoners was carried out over the course of a full week. Although the lopping off of heads lasted a mere forty minutes, the full effect of those forty minutes would last a thousand years to anyone with thoughts of causing harm to the powerful Caesar. Normally, the pirates, and every inhabitant of the village would have been wiped off the face of the earth. In this case, however, Caesar spared the villagers in order to serve a greater purpose. They became the most effective propagandists of Caesar's message: "If you attack Rome, you will meet a horrific end."

When Caesar returned to Rome, he returned the ransom that had been paid to gain his own freedom. A portion of the ransom money could not be recovered, so he personally paid the missing sum back from his own substantial accounts."

Captain Woodes Rogers gave a firm nod, indicating to the king that he understood the meaning of the story. The king concluded the story and sharing his greater purpose in the telling of the tale.

"I tell you this tale because I believe that it is relevant to your upcoming journey. We can learn from this tale. You must not rush your planning. Take the necessary time in calculating the steps to garner success. Out-think the pirates. Show no mercy to the scoundrels who choose not to accept my pardon. Make examples of those opposing my empire. Let the outcome of their opposition to England and the breaking of her laws send a clear message: if you are the enemy of England, you will suffer. Reinforce this message by displaying the bodies of those you execute, just as Caesar did.

"Captain Rogers, I can see that you are a fine choice for this post. Once all arrangements have been made, I will announce your commission as the Royal Governor of the Bahamas."

"Your Highness, with God's grace and the blessing of the

British Empire, we shall advance another step toward winning the race we spoke of earlier,"

As the king had stated, on the fifth day of January 1718, a proclamation was issued announcing clemency for all piratical offences, provided that those seeking the "King's Pardon" surrendered no later than the fifth day of September 1718. All colonial governors and deputy governors were authorized to grant the pardon. Rogers was officially appointed Captain General and Governor in Chief by King George on the sixth day of January 1718.

Being newly appointed governor, Rogers understands that this is his biggest opportunity to make his mark. If successful, he will become wealthy and immortalized in historical records for centuries. When he was younger and less experienced, he would have prepared and moved quickly to reach his destination. Rogers is older now and more experienced. Rather than rushing to his new post, he heeds the king's advice and spends months preparing for his expedition.

He meticulously plans everything down to its last detail. This expedition will include seven ships, each manned by a full crew, one hundred soldiers, and one hundred and thirty colonists. Supplies will range from food for the expedition's members and crews to religious pamphlets to distribute among the pirates. On the twenty-second day of April 1718, the expedition set sail from London, pulling away from the docks on the River Thames just in time to catch the afternoon tide.

CHAPTER TEN

THE WHITE DEVILS

In the early 1700s, anyone living in most European cities could take a casual stroll to the market in the central square to choose and buy a wide variety of fruits, vegetables and fresh meats. Alternatively, for a bit of socializing, a nice selection of stews, breads and cooked meats could always be found at pubs and inns that occupied virtually every corner. Finding sustenance in a West African tribal village, on the other hand, depended wholly on the tribe's ability to gather enough food to feed every man, woman, and child.

It's early morning as five young tribesmen gather their weapons and hunting gear. They wear very little clothing— only a modest piece of cloth or well-tanned and softened animal hide that efficiently covers their genitals. One of the men begins handing the others' bota bags, preserved zebra stomachs made into canteens, each holding enough water to sustain the hunters throughout the hot, dry day.

The sun has just risen above the eastern horizon as the hunters prepare to leave their village. The temperature at this early hour will only grow warmer until night comes again and cools the wilderness. The oldest tribesman in this hunting party, a tall and muscular man named Ajani tells the others that it is time to leave. As he looks back at the still sleeping village, all he hears are the continual humming sounds of locusts and an occasional bark from one of the village dogs.

The hunting party passes through the village's perimeter fence, which is constructed of tightly woven thorn bushes, tree branches and vines of various sizes. Barriers of this type are common among all African villages and are erected to provide protection against large wandering herds of buffalo, elephant, and wildebeest. The barricade also protects the tribe against larger nocturnal predators such as lions, leopards, and hyenas.

This group of men is only one of four hunting parties that venture out daily into the African wilderness, hunting to feed their village. As the men hunt, the women gather roots, tubers, and berries and fill containers with fresh water. This ritual is repeated daily in order to survive.

The hunting party has spent hours tracking a number of animals without a kill. They pick up fresh tracks of a crested porcupine and follow them to the doorway of its burrow. The men know that trapping the animal there does not mean it will be any easier to kill it. They know exactly what needs to be done and begin digging. They take turns and dig feverishly, following the path of the hole that the creature has created. After digging four and a half feet straight down, the burrow changes direction.

Now the youngest tribesman begins digging horizontally. He suddenly freezes. Thinking he might have heard the animal, he pauses and motions for silence. They know that cornering a porcupine in its burrow will make it more dangerous. As he pauses, he hears the creature's aggressive warning: stamping its feet, clicking its teeth, and growling while vibrating its quills producing a threatening rattling sound. The man quietly kneels and lays belly-down on the moist soil in an attempt to spot the animal holding its ground in the pitch black hole.

The young man understands that the closer he gets to the animal, the more at-risk he becomes. He makes sure to point the sharp iron barb of his spear toward the dark opening. As the hunter pokes and jabs his spear into the burrow, he sees the hind end of the porcupine as it rushes out of the darkness and turns around into the attack position. Before the young hunter has time to react, the animal raises itself up and in an instant releases a fusillade of sharp, rock-hard quills.

The animal only weighs forty pounds and is less than three feet long, but its hundreds of footlong quills present a formidable defense and more than compensate for the creature's smallish size. When the quill tips penetrate, their barbs lodge into the flesh like fishhooks and are difficult to pull out, causing pain. The young man panics and jumps out of the hole in an instant. The others laugh as the boy tries to calm himself, working to calm the sudden surge of adrenaline flowing through his body.

Having coaxed the animal from its burrow, the oldest hunter, Ajani expertly launches his spear into the porcupine's body, killing it instantly. He then instructs two of the younger men to skin the animal and remove its quills. In minutes, they throw its bare and meaty carcass into a coarsely woven sack.

As the hunting party returns with their game, they hear several loud booming noises. The group stops and stands frozen as they begin to see smoke rising toward the sky in the distance. As if choreographed, the men simultaneously cast off their canteens, toss their dead game to the ground and begin running. With spears in hand, they intensify their pace as they hear their women screaming and men yelling. As they draw closer, it becomes clear their village is under attack. Two of the five men begin screaming wildly, running full-bore into the violence. Ajani does not follow. He takes cover within a thicket of tall grass outside the village's barricade to observe what is taking place. He must size up the situation before fully committing himself to action.

Hearing a noise over his left shoulder, Ajani turns quickly with his spear poised to kill. He recognizes the two younger men from his hunting party. They followed him, the most experienced warrior, into the grass. Ajani uses his head and spear in a silent motion ordering them to run away. They take off in the opposite direction of their village, staying low as they run through the field of tall grass. Ajani moves closer to determine where best to strike the enemy.

The dust from the disturbed ground that surrounds his village is thick in the air. Sweat pours from his body as the ground bleeds off its searing heat, creating visible heat waves that distort his vision. Ajani rushes behind a patch of Hawthorn bushes growing near a large fallen tree. He hears screaming women, yelling men and a loud booming that emanates from the wooden and metal sticks the raiders carry.

Ajani sees two of his tribe's women, in a full sprint, three men chasing them. Two of the men hurl a net over one of the women and a corner of it catches the feet of another causing her to fall hard to the ground. Ajani now knows that these men are the white devils his tribe has heard about. Neighboring tribes on the west coast of Africa have been passing along warnings for more than two years. They say that these strange men come in large ships and raid their villages. Not for food or valuables, but for people.

The raiders take most as prisoners and the rest, they kill. The few tribesmen lucky enough not to be captured say these white men speak in strange tongues and are believed to be the devil's soldiers, hunting people to feed their souls. Those who are taken never return.

These men are, in fact, Portuguese sailors who capture slaves and ferry them across the Atlantic to the New World in horrendous conditions on one of three legs of the Trans-Atlantic "Golden Triangle." The yearlong voyages are designed for pure profit—setting sail from west Africa, holds packed with human cargo and human misery, the ships follow the trade winds westward to the New World—the

Caribbean—where, as slaves, they are worked to near death on sugar plantations. The ships' masters then head north to the English colonies along the east coast of North America. Here, they offload sugar and spices and load their foul holds with tobacco, cotton and other commodities. Finally, they follow the Gulf Stream back across the North Atlantic to eager buyers in England.

The two men work feverishly to gain full control of the captured women who fight back ferociously. Ajani makes a break for a dense thicket of trees nearly forty yards away. As he readies himself for the sprint, drawing in deep breaths and squatting down for a fast and furious dash, he closes his eyes and mouths a silent prayer. As he runs for the trees, he remains as low as possible, the fallen tree shielding him from the raiders, obstructing their view as well as muffling any sounds he makes as his feet move swiftly across the ground.

He hears one of the men yell but does not look back. Without warning, more of the white devils jump from behind the trees and snare Ajani in their net. Ajani rolls violently as a blinding wave of fear hits him. The men hold the net down on all sides and begin to twist the net tightly around Ajani's body as he struggles. However, the combination of Ajani's panicked twisting and turning only tightens the grip of the net. He struggles to the point of exhaustion as his sweat mixes with the dust and dirt. His skin is covered with a muddy layer of his ancestors' earth.

Finally, Ajani ceases his fight and resigns himself to his fate. Barely able to move, he turns his head enough to see his captors, the devils who will now surely allow their souls to feed upon him. The sun is directly behind them and all Ajani can see are silhouettes. As he lies entangled in the net, struggling to control his breathing and find some way to loosen its constricting hold, he recalls the words of his father, who told him his name, Ajani, means, *He who wins the struggle*. Ajani glances once more at the big man who leads those standing over him. He sees him raise the butt of his weapon and begin a fierce downward swing.

Ajani's entire world goes dark.

Chapter Eleven

Burleson's Property

Ajani survives the long voyage across the Atlantic. Many are not as lucky. The prisoners live in the ship's cargo hold, stacked side-by-side, on three-and-a-half by six-foot wooden platforms approximately six inches off the floor and chained to iron blocks secured tightly to the ship's hull. With no sunlight, little food and no facilities to relieve themselves, the human cargo exists only inches from a cesspool of human waste. At times, the seas are rough. Many become seasick, creating a putrid mixture of vomit, urine and feces covering the entire floor. Many die of dysentery, some from other diseases and others from self-induced starvation.

Others die when the ship's quartermaster informs the Capitan that transporting more human cargo than expected would cause food supplies to run dangerously low before reaching their destination. The captain has no choice but to reduce the number of mouths to feed and orders the vessel's master and crew to tie a half-dozen prisoners together, include heavy iron or even a cannonball, and then push them from the deck into the sea. As their bodies plunge into the cold water, the weight of the iron pulls them quickly downward into the depths. Panic for survival overtakes most as they frantically try to free themselves, while some, resigned to their fate, calmly stare at each other in horror until the seas grow black.

The ship's cargo doors are flung open, sending a blinding light into the eyes of the Africans, who have not seen sunlight in weeks. The Portuguese use the sunlight to disorient the prisoners temporarily. Captives who have been temporarily blinded are more easily managed and less likely to react. They are led from the ship, across the street and into a large stone building used to hold captives before they are transported to market. Ajani and his people are placed in a dark, damp room beneath the building where they will be cleaned and prepared for auction.

When the Portuguese ship finally arrives in Charles Towne, Ajani has lost thirty pounds from his muscular frame. He is weakened, but after being rinsed, he still looks reasonably healthy and strong. The auctioneer visits the docks to inspect all cargo that will be brought to market, assessing the potential value of each. After his inspection, he determines the starting bid for each item. Some members of the human cargo are worth more than others are. The starting bid for frail or sickly slaves is much lower in an attempt to move the slave trader's inventory, the cargo that fared better than others is considered more valuable. He enters the room outside the cell and each slave is brought before him. A guard watches for any sudden movements that would suggest the slave intends to escape or cause harm to anyone.

As Ajani is brought to stand facing the auctioneer, the guard orders, "Esteja ainda!" Ajani does not understand the Portuguese language. He has no idea what the guard has just said. He hears the tone of the guard's voice and guesses he has been told to stand still. He looks at the portly man sitting at the table in front of him. He pays no attention to Ajani as he uses a bird's feather to mark on a tan sheet. The man then moves around the table and stands before Ajani. He looks Ajani up and down, and then commands, "Abra sua boca!" The man picks up a footlong wooden dowel and firmly presses it downward against Ajani's chin. Ajani opens his mouth as the man begins to inspect Ajani's teeth. He then pushes the dowel against Ajani's stomach, arms and legs to check Ajani's muscle tone. He shakes his head in a positive motion and sits back down behind his table. After marking the sheet, he says, "Excelente. Eu sou terminado. Traga-me seguinte." Ajani is then led back into the cell with the others.

While in the holding room, Ajani begins looking for fellow captives who know his native Bantu language. He finds a slightly older man taken from a neighboring village near the same time and asks him, "What will come of us?"

The older African pauses for a moment before responding, "I have heard that we will be made the property of other men."

As Ajani thinks about what has just been said, he asks the man, "How can a man be owned by another? You mean we are to be traded as we trade for animals back home?"

"Yes, like animals."

Ajani and the others spend only one night and a half-day in the holding room before being marched into a large courtyard located in the center of the complex. He looks around to find that twelve-foot-high stone walls surround the courtyard. Armed men watch from on top. Any thoughts of escape leave his mind. One by one, each African is marched onto a stagelike wooden platform, where they are displayed to the waiting crowd and sold to their new owners. Most are sold to plantations needing field hands. Ajani is led to the platform. He is displayed wearing only a modest loincloth. Before being taken from the holding cell, he is put in chains and shackles by the guard to prevent him from attempting escape. A slave woman then rubs oil onto the bodies of only selected men. This accentuates the muscles of the younger and stronger men. The traders and auctioneers know that if these men are presented properly to the bidding crowd, they will command much more money than that of the average African. While on the platform, Ajani looks into a sea of white-skinned people as the auctioneer babbles loudly in a strange language. He notices that men are raising their hands subtly in a response to the man behind him. The man shouts in excitement and causes Ajani to flinch as he is startled by the sound of the auctioneer slamming his gavel hard onto a block of wood. As quickly as the auctioneer yells, *"SOLD to Collin Burleson!"* Ajani is loaded with two others into a wagon bound for their new home. Ajani has been sold to Collin Burleson, the owner of a tobacco plantation north of Charles Towne. The Burleson plantation has been growing the finest flue-cured tobacco in Carolina, its operations in existence for three generations. Collin Burleson has been around tobacco his entire life, inheriting everything, just as his father did years ago from Collin's grandfather.

CHAPTER TWELVE

ELY'S WHIP

During summer, the temperature in Carolina rarely climbs above ninety degrees, but this summer has been unusually hot. The slaves have been suffering through one of the hottest in memory. Today is the sixteenth consecutive day above one hundred degrees and is expected to be even hotter.

On any Southern plantation, all slaves are expected to work from sunup to sundown. When brought to the Burleson plantation, the owner gives them new names in order to strip them of any past identities. With a new name and different home, they enter into a new life without the families and friends from which they have been stolen. Ajani is now named Carrick, an English name of which Master Burleson has always been fond.

The new arrivals are taken into the main barn where they are told to stand in a line. Ajani and two others can feel the heat emanating from a mound of intensely burning red-hot coals in front of them. Two men grab the arms of the first slave and lead him closer to the burning coals. A man with a large mustache and muttonchops enters the barn, stands next to the coals and grabs a metal rod that's been heated to a shimmering red-white glow. The two men force the slave down to his knees as muttonchops grabs one leg. He takes the branding iron from the coals and presses it firmly against the slave's calf. The sound of skin sizzling followed quickly by a loud cry of pain and the pungent smell of burnt flesh fills the air.

Ajani's heart races as he is forced to his knees. He is determined not to cry out in pain. As the branding iron is inches away from his calf, he feels the intense heat near his skin. As the white hot metal makes contact, the pain is too great and Ajani lets out a sharp yell. The men are branded to mark them permanently as the property of the Burleson plantation. It will blister and result in a highly visible, raised scar of the letter "B."

Life on the plantation is harsh. Although the field hands are well fed at the end of each day. The heat is relentless. It reminds Ajani of the summers growing up in his village in Africa, but there he had not been working twelve to fifteen hours every day, under the constant threat of a bullwhip biting sharply into his back.

Ajani has been a slave for two months and has constant thoughts of escaping to find his way back home. He knows that any attempt during the day will be nearly impossible.

The slaves are under constant watch by the plantation's overseer, Ely Harrison. After dark, all new slaves are bunked together in small cabins that are securely locked, preventing nighttime escape. Only the slaves who have been working on the plantation for years, resigning themselves to a lifetime of slavery, have the freedom to visit with each other outside their cabins during evening hours.

As the summer days get longer and hotter, Harrison becomes harder on the field hands. Some of the slaves working in the tobacco fields fall to heat stroke and dehydration. If a slave languishes in the heat, Harrison would much rather motivate a quick return to work with a painful crack of his bullwhip than show compassion or provide care. He views Master Burleson's slaves as property—a means to grow, cultivate and harvest tobacco crops—nothing more.

After working the fields for ten hours, one of the slave women falls to her knees. As she begins to fade, Ajani, only a few feet away, looks to see Harrison firmly mounted atop his horse, with his back turned to Ajani and the heat-stricken woman, keeping watch on the others. Ajani hears the man barking out orders. Knowing that he has only a few seconds to get the woman off the ground, he rushes over and grabs her from behind lifting her onto her feet.

Ajani hears Harrison yell out, "You there!" and sees the horse quickly moving in his direction. As Ajani lifts the woman, he turns to see the horse bearing down on them, only feet away. The overseer uses the horse as a battering ram and, without hesitation, smashes the thirteen hundred pound animal into the two slaves.

The woman and Ajani land ten feet away on tobacco plants, breaking the stalks and delicate leaves. The other slaves momentarily halt their work to see what is taking place. The woman is unconscious. As he lies on the ground, Ajani raises his head, spitting blood and dirt. The overseer positions his horse to provide the best angle to use his bullwhip on Ajani, whipping him viciously, the leather cracking with each swing.

Ajani feels the sting of Ely's whip cut into his lower back and thighs. He cries out loudly in pain and anger. The whip hits his face and wraps around his upper torso. He grabs hold of the whip, and pulls with all his strength, causing Ely to slide backward halfway off his saddle. The struggle spooks the horse, causing it to panic, whinnying and rearing up, causing Ely to lose his balance completely and fall awkwardly to the ground. He hits with a loud thud but quickly jumps to his feet. Noticing that Ajani is now holding his bullwhip, Ely says, "Got the whip do you, you stupid son-of-a-bitch?" and begins to reach for his pistol. Ajani sees his hand moving toward the handle of his flintlock.

Without hesitation, he lunges toward Ely and slams him to the ground, quickly straddling his chest. Ely's back is against the ground, and his arms are locked beneath Ajani's legs. He desperately struggles to force Ajani off his chest. Still holding Ely's whip, he presses its leather-wrapped handle firmly against Ely's throat. The white man's eyes widen as he realizes that he is only seconds away from death. In desperation, he yells out to the other slaves, "Help me! Damn you ... help me!"

After being beaten and abused by Harrison time and again, his plead falls on deaf ears. The other slaves keep their heads down, eyes focused on their work and do nothing to help him. Ely begins to kick his legs frantically in a last-ditch effort to free himself from Ajani's control. Ajani looks into his eyes and says, "Lazima kufa!" (You must die!), before using the weight of his body to easily push down on the whip's handle, crushing Ely's windpipe and breaking his neck. The trauma severs his spinal cord causing instant paralysis. Ely lies completely motionless on top of the crushed tobacco plants. Ajani watches as Ely slowly dies of asphyxiation.

Knowing what he has just done, Ajani stands over Ely's body and throws the whip to the ground. He looks around at all his fellow slaves, who are staring at him in shock. He sees one of the older slaves pointing in the opposite direction of the Burleson Plantation and motions for him to run. Ajani begins through the tobacco field not stopping for miles. Finally, he stops to catch his breath and get his bearings. In his panic, he did not look to see in which direction he was headed. He knows he will have only until sunset before Ely's body is discovered dead in the field.

Ajani also knows that he is not only a runaway slave, but also the murderer of a white man. He will be hunted like an animal and, if found, killed on the spot. His only hope is to disappear. His first task is to distance himself quickly from the Burleson Plantation.

Ajani runs parallel to the road that delivered him into slavery only months earlier. He is careful to stay out of sight of passing travelers. He knows this road will lead him away from the plantation and to the ocean. After running for hours, his body cannot keep pace with the demands placed on it. His powerful leg muscles have atrophied during the long weeks shackled deep in the bowels of the slave ship.

He feels an intense burning in his legs. His arms grow heavy. His lungs feel as if they will burst. As exhaustion sets in, his brain sends messages commanding him to stop. He now sees the Atlantic Ocean in the distance and continues to push his body on. The only thing greater than his intense pain is his will to survive.

As the moments pass, he draws closer to the water. He hears the sound of waves meeting the shore. The grassy field gives way to the sandy shoreline. He staggers and collapses. In a semi-delirious state, he rolls onto his back, lies motionless and watches the sky turn colorful shades of yellow, orange and purple as the sun begins to set. He closes his eyes for a moment in an attempt to focus on his breathing.

As he lies on the sand, he sees the look in Ely's eyes at the moment that he crushed his neck. The thought causes him to roll over abruptly and bend up onto his knees. Ajani releases an angered cry as he slowly gains the strength to return to his feet. Surveying his surroundings, he spots several ships anchored offshore. He realizes that the sand dunes and tall grass that surround him will provide him cover and conceal his presence as he continues to follow the shoreline toward the ships and his possible escape.

By the time Ajani reaches the Port of Charles Towne, darkness has fallen. He is certain that, after the discovery of Ely's body and his own absence, the authorities will take immediate action. Likely, they were notified hours ago and are already positioned at all possible escape routes. He will have to board one of the anchored ships secretly, hide himself below deck and hope for the best.

Ajani lingers in the shadows weaving in and out of the buildings that line the docks. He spots a large merchant ship with men working feverishly, unloading cargo and readying the ship to set sail. He works his way to the shoreline, enters the cool water and swims silently toward the backside of the ship. He bides his time for the opportunity to make his move.

When the crew is out of sight, he climbs one of the large ropes that secure the ship tightly to the dock, using all of his remaining strength. Onboard, he hides below deck in the darkest spot he can find behind cargo. Ajani waits patiently as the ship sets sail for New Providence.

CHAPTER THIRTEEN

A KING'S PARDON

Jack Rackham tucks his loose silk shirt into his brightly colored pants and places his large tricorn hat atop his head as he leaves Nancy dressing in their rented room. Opening the inn's front door, he steps into the bright Caribbean sun. He pauses for a moment, looks up to the sun, and takes in a deep breath of the sea air. He has been captain of his ship and crew for only two-and-a-half weeks and has been back on land for three of those days.

Just a month ago, he had been quartermaster on Captain Charles Vane's ship, the *Ranger*. Vane, like other pirate captains, used New Providence as his base of operations. He was extremely popular with his crew. Not only did he have an uncanny ability to find treasure-laden ships for the taking, but also was a charismatic, natural leader. However, Vane also had a dark side. On a number of occasions, Jack and the *Ranger*'s crew had witnessed him cruelly torturing captives.

Jack believes that Vane truly enjoyed killing other men and watching them suffer while rationalizing his actions as being necessary in forcing the prisoners to confess where they had hidden valuables aboard. He killed one man with his bare hands, beating him to a bloody pulp. He frequently tortured other captives in more cruel and unimaginable ways. Jack remembers seeing Vane's eyes during these episodes—black as coal and showing no emotion.

One day, a sailor perched high in the crow's nest spotted a ship approaching off their starboard bow. Vane and his crew had happened upon a French Man-o'-War. Vane chose not to attack the well-armed ship, figuring that its plunder was not worth the risk. His crew was outraged by his decision and saw it as an act of cowardice. When his position as captain was put to a vote, Vane lost. Along with six of his supporters, he was put into a longboat and cast adrift. Rackham was voted captain less than an hour later.

Now captain of the vessel, Jack announces the new name of the ship as *The Vanity*, further reinforcing the ship's change in command. Jack inherits a 65-foot, 113-ton Dutch-designed sloop built by Jamaican master craftsmen with a capacity to sail at a top speed of over 10 knots. The ship is capable of manning a crew of seventy men. Experienced sailors know that the tried-and-true Dutch design, combined with Jamaican shipbuilding techniques, equates to a superior vessel that is both seaworthy and fast. Jamaican shipyards built these vessels of red cedar, which makes for stout, sturdy craft.

The former captain had elected to strip down the ship's interior bulkheads to provide more space for the crew and to give them the ability to carry extra guns. He also opted not to add more of the typical six- to eight-pound guns that the ship was designed to carry. Instead, Vane had the ship retrofitted to carry a combination of twelve-pounders and heavier eighteen-pound guns, giving it a powerful combination of increased firepower and longer cannon range, enabling it to outgun many ships while still being able to launch lightning-swift attacks.

The ship's speed allows it to outrun larger and heavier pursuers if needed. And its draft, amazingly shallow at eight feet, finds safety in shallower waters—far beyond the reach of heavier warships.

Jack walks toward the dozen or so crewmen gathered near the seafront docks, where *The Vanity* and several other ships are securely tied off. As he approaches the men, he hears concern in their voices. One of the men says, (with his back to Jack and only feet away), "British Man-o'-War ships coming here…"

Sensing obvious concern in the voices of his men, Jack enters the conversation on a lighter note. He pretends not to have heard their conversation, and in an authoritative voice but with a flippant tone says, "Lads, there are two things that I love most in life, the dimples on a naked woman's lower back and being the captain of *The Vanity*. Judging from the quiver in your voices I heard as I approached, the devil himself must be coming to visit us."

The men turn to address Jack. The ship's Quartermaster, Richard Corner replies, "Not the devil, captain, but the British."

"The British? Why can't those red-coated bastards leave things be without having to poke their heads into matters that don't concern them?"

One of Jack's shipmates replies, "Aye, Captain Rackham, sounds a tad worse than the Brits just stopping by for shore leave and a night of drinking our rum."

Jack's face turns more serious as he asks, "Lads, what have you heard? And divulge your source."

One of the well-dressed locals, the former privateer and merchant Morris Cooper, addresses him, saying, "Jack, the source is myself."

"Indeed? Well, Sir Cooper, might I ask how this news came to you?"

"From the third ship in front of us that docked late last evening, when all were enjoying their rum in the Goat's Head Tavern. A letter was hand-delivered to me by a courier under the authority of the king himself. Jack, with all due respect to your command, I can only speculate that the letter was delivered to me knowing that I made my fortune long ago and am now a permanent fixture here—one of the few respected citizens who still enjoys the company of rogues such as yourself."

"So, man, tell me of this letter's contents."

"The letter was so damned official that when reading it, I

nearly soiled myself. Since declaring this region and its people loyal subjects to the crown, King George has appointed Woodes Rogers the First Royal Governor of the Bahamas. Incidentally, I know this gent. He, his brother and crew sailed together as privateers years ago, when I was at the end of my career. He was made famous by commanding an expedition that circumnavigated the globe, returning with his two original ships and a large Spanish galleon taken as a prize.

Although his younger brother was killed, he returned with most of his crew, not to mention a king's ransom from the ships he had taken during his voyage. It appears that he has traded privateering for a career in politics and has landed a post to rule over us. He, his men, colonists and a fleet of ships are expected to arrive in a matter of days."

"Tell me what more you know of this Brit."

"Well, Jack, I do know that this man is of tough character, and when he sets his mind to something, he would rather go to his grave than give up. During a battle with the Spanish, he was shot in the face and foot. Even with his jawbone shattered, pieces of a musket ball lodged in the roof of his mouth and half his heel blown-off, he managed to capture one Spanish ship laden with treasures and continued chasing and battling the second, larger Spanish ship for days before having to retreat."

"I assume that he's been sent here for us?"

"Not *us*, Jack, but *you*, and the other pirate captains and their crews that call New Providence home. However, this letter comes with both an offer and a threat. The offer is that all pirates operating in this region will receive a full pardon for the crime of piracy if they join England to fight as privateers against her enemies, Spain and France."

"And the threat?"

"Any person practicing piracy in the region from this day forward will be breaking laws set forth by King George and the British Commonwealth. Those caught breaking these laws will be tried for piracy. Convicted, you and others would be hanged."

"So mighty England and its puppet, Woodes Rogers, intend to invade our home and try to control us under a Letter of Marque?"

CHAPTER FOURTEEN

THE VOTE

Jack despises the fact that the British are on their way to Nassau. He asks himself, "Who the bloody hell does this Woodes Rogers think he is, telling us what we can and cannot do?" As captain, Jack has the unwavering obedience of his men, knowing they would lay down their lives for him in battle. However, the unwritten-yet-all-powerful pirate code allows that other non-wartime decisions can be made by a vote of the ship's crew, and he must address the issue with them. Jack's vote in these situations counts only as one, no more or less valuable than that of the lowliest ship's boy living in the squalor in the foc'sle "before the mast."

Jack orders a few of his men to spread the word that he has set orders for all hands to meet aboard the ship. He has thought very carefully about what he will say—the all-important words he will use—and how to best present their options. He has not been captain long, but knows that if handled right, this situation can be used to bolster his image as captain and galvanize his command. In his cabin he imagines all of the potential scenarios and rehearses how he would look, act and sound giving orders to his crew.

His memory is still fresh regarding the circumstances that made him captain—and the actions his crew took against his predecessor. Jack knows that if he were to show the slightest sign of weakness, he would also be cast adrift to die, as were Charles Vane and the motley crew who tossed in their lot with him. By now, it is dark, with barely a sliver of a moon hanging in the sky. All of Jack's men are aboard, waiting for him to emerge from his private quarters beneath the poop deck and address them.

He dresses in his finest clothes before leaving his cabin and stepping out onto the ship's main deck to address his crew. He stands and looks at the faces that stand illuminated by the flickering torches that surround them. He walks silently—slowly and confidently—in order to build tension and anticipation for what he is about to say.

Every movement, gesture and word has been thoroughly choreographed. As he slowly paces, he stops at his cabin door and turns slowly to face his men.

In a deep and bellowing voice he begins, "Men, I know by now you've heard that the British will soon be joining us here in New Providence." The crew let out a muffled grumble. "It would seem that our new guv-nuh, a man named Woodes Rogers, is headed this way, with the intention to bring law and order to this region and keep us under the king's thumb." The mumbles shifted to a snide laughter. Jack paused before proceeding. "The good guv-nuh was considerate enough to send a letter in advance of his arrival announcing the monarchy's intentions, which delivers both a proposition and a threat. This is not a wartime decision. You, the crew, must cast your votes and decide what we will do.

"It seems that this Rogers fellow has seen fit to give us an ultimatum before even the courtesy of a stern warning. Lads, here is what's in front of us: His Majesty demands that all who practice piracy from this isle and region fight with England as privateers. We would take up arms against England's enemies, Spain and France. If we choose not to privateer for the Crown, the expectation is that we would give up our trade altogether in exchange for an honest man's living. By taking them up on their proposition, a full pardon would be granted to all." The crew mumbles, each man casting a glance at shipmates to the right and left.

"This proposition would see us sharing our prize with investors who would sponsor our raids. There is more. We would give up our right to choose targets as we see fit. The threat is, if we choose to remain on the account, England will proclaim us her enemy, and if caught, our necks will surely be stretched on the gallows."

Jack looks out at the faces staring back at him, shadows dancing in the light of the flickering torches. He hears his men talking in low voices among themselves. One of the deckhands yells out, "Damn the bloody Brits." The remainder of the crew chimes in with a roar echoing the seaman's sentiments if only to ease the tension each feels in the hollow of his gut. Jack, casting a long, slow glance from beam to beam, continues.

"Lads, I do not mean to sway your votes either way. However, as your captain, I would like to tell you how I view our predicament. After the Spanish abandoned New Providence, free-minded gentlemen such as us claimed this jewel as our own. We've been here for years. I take a strong exception to anyone, including God's almighty England, deciding on a whim that they wish to lay claim to what I see as ours.

"I find it arrogant and naive that the Brits would assume that we would give up our way of life to fight with them as an ally against their enemies. I, for one, am more inclined to join the opposition and become an enemy of England." The crew stood silently, absorbing the captain's words of treason.

"Now, tell me how you see it by the votes ye cast." Jack turns from his crew, who watches his every move, climbing the ladder to the poop deck to stand beside the enormous wheel. The crew takes mere moments to decide. They will continue under Jack's command, appointing the ship's bosun to deliver their verdict. As Jack is given the results of the vote, he lets out a confident and spontaneous laugh turning to the quartermaster, Richard Corner, and the ship's navigator, George Featherston. "Misters Corner and Featherston, call all hands to ready the ship for sail. Inform the crew that we shall leave New Providence on tomorrow's evening tide."

Corner and Featherston snap to a pirate's attention and reply loudly enough for the crew—now loitering about the main deck—to hear, "Aye, aye, captain."

"Oh, and Mister Corner, one more thing, when speaking to the crew, I noticed a foremaster that I do not know, the tall black man there, standing amid the provisions. Who might he be?"

"Captain, that man went on the account just two days back. He calls himself Ajani. We reckon he found his way to us aboard one of the merchant ships that arrived the other day from, Norfolk, Charles Towne, or Philadelphia. He is likely on the run from a slave owner. He speaks gibberish, no English and understands nothing of ships. He shows a bit of hesitancy to go below, sir. An odd thing."

Jack interrupts, "Ah, perfect. He shall sail with us. We will teach him all the English that he needs, and he will learn only what we want him to know about ships. We can make use of his strong back, and I imagine that in the heat of battle he looks like the devil himself."

Chapter Fifteen

Welcoming Committee

As the ship is provisioned and readied to sail, Richard Corner and George Featherston join Jack in his spacious quarters at the vessel's stern to roughly plot their course. Jack says, "Following the coastline of the British colonies should give us a bounty of ships to choose from. The merchant ships coming and going will keep us busy." It is midafternoon when their planning is interrupted. Hearing one of his crew members call out, and based on the urgency within the cry, he has a fairly good idea what the commotion is all about. *The British.*

Woodes Rogers and his fleet of ships are spotted a half-mile from shore. Jack and his crew are only a few hours from cutting ties and leaving New Providence. With seven British ships entering the harbor, Jack knows that he will get a good look at them on the way out to sea. The British ships drop their anchors after entering the mouth of the harbor preparing their crew to go ashore. Using his spyglass, he gets a better view of each ship from a distance. The polished brass beauty was lifted from a Dutch captain's quarters after taking over the merchant vessel nearly a week ago.

"The new guv-nuh has arrived with two man-o'-war, four frigates, and a cargo ship. It looks as though he has brought half of bloody England with him."

As Jack lowers his spyglass, he pivots on one heel to face his crew and gives a short grunt that comes from the innermost burrows of his rum-plated diaphragm. He orders his men to assemble and lend a firm ear. They immediately gather and listen intently as their captain instructs them. "Men, our plan is to sail from New Providence and up the colonial coast. You all voted as I did, to remain on the account. As you can see, we will pass the new guv-nuh and his seven ships. I'm sure they will be keeping as close an eye on us as we will them. On our way out to search for our fortunes, I will get a closer look at this Woodes Rogers chap. I want to make sure that Calico Jack Rackham and his crew on *The Vanity* make a suitable impression on the king's hired dog."

Jack yells to his navigator, "Mister Featherston, I want *The Vanity* to pass less than a ship's length broadside of that lead man-o'-war. I want our wake to topple what's not nailed down."

"Is that all, captain?"

"Have the mates below deck ready all cannons with full loads of bar shot. Tell the lads to keep all gun ports closed until my order is given to open fire."

"Captain Rackham, do we intend to bring the fight to the British?"

"We will see how they respond to us first. If they fire upon us, we'll sink them where they are anchored. Oh, and Mister Corner, do not raise our flag. I don't want them to know our intentions. It'll be best to keep them guessing."

"Aye, aye, captain."

During his younger years, Jack served with the Royal Navy's merchant fleet as a deckhand and navigator. He was well trained in battle strategies, tactics and maritime protocols. As *The Vanity* begins sailing toward the anchored British fleet, Jack calls upon his instinctive knowledge. He quickly thinks through the dynamics of the situation: *British protocol dictates that all officers of the Royal Navy weigh on the side of caution and not open fire unless they are certain that there is an obvious threat. By this time, the Brits will have identified us as Dutch, not an enemy of England. They will also have noticed that we are sailing without a flag, which should cause brief confusion and indecision, as they will not know if we pose a threat. Sailing directly toward their position, in such close proximity, will put them on guard and they will ready their guns for firing. If the British were to open fire on us broadside at such close range, we would surely be blown out of the water, but the Brits will also assume that a single ship would not dare consider attacking an opposing force that outnumbers it seven-to-one. No, they will not attack. They will simply stand on their decks and look dumbfounded as we sail past.*

As *The Vanity* nears the lead British ship, Jack looks and sees their crew scrambling, their gun ports opening, and cannons being pointed in his direction. He begins to wonder if his calculated, unorthodox idea to prop his image as a fearless captain would be a critical error that could cost him and his crew their lives. The crew of *The Vanity* also prepares for battle, adrenaline suddenly spiked. As they begin to draw near the British man-o'-war, Jack tells Corner, "Quartermaster, have the men bellow their favorite shanty loud and clear as we approach, and once we are fifty yards away from that ship, have them stop and remain completely silent as we start to pass her."

Meanwhile, on the British ship, the quartermaster knocks on Rogers' cabin door. As the door opens the quartermaster says, "Governor, pardon the intrusion, but a Dutch sloop is headed directly toward us."

"Do they fly Dutch colors?"

"No, sir, they sail with no flag."

"Let's take a look, shall we?"

Rogers walks swiftly and confidently across his ship's deck to get a better look at the approaching sloop. *The Vanity* is now less than three hundred yards from Rogers' ship. Rogers gives his quartermaster a stern look in silence before asking him in an irate tone, "Why did you wait so bloody long to inform me? That ship is nearly on top of us!"

The quartermaster anxiously mutters, "Sir, I was" …

Rogers interrupts and yells, "Silence! Hand me my spyglass now and have the bosun pipe the crew to general quarters!" The quartermaster obediently hands his captain a spyglass. After taking a long glance, Rogers says, "No flag and the gun ports are closed. Quartermaster, do we have our ports open and cannons readied?"

"Aye, we do."

"Well then, make sure the men below are ready and prepared to fire on my order."

Rogers and his men hear the crew on the approaching Dutch ship singing loudly. Jack orders the helmsman to swing the rudder gently ten points to starboard to bring his ship perfectly broadside as it approaches within a hundred yards.

Rogers shouts, "Ready to fire on my order!"

Jack quickly makes his way down the ladder from the poop deck to the portside railing so that he will have the best vantage point to see Rogers and for Rogers to see him. *The Vanity* is now close enough for Rogers' orders to be heard by all. All aboard are certain they are on the verge of battle. The crew stops singing. Tension grows. All becomes deathly quiet as *The Vanity* slowly begins to pass the man-o'-war. The only sound to be heard is the gentle lap of her hull cutting through the water. The navigator steers the ship even closer as they pass.

Jack places one hand onto the ships taffrail and props one

foot up on the ship's side railing. He sees a man looking directly at him and knows that this must be Rogers. Rogers sees a man dressed in brightly colored clothes and wearing a black tricorn hat, with a large red plume, staring right back at him. The two ships are directly abeam of each other now, only forty yards apart. At their closest point, Jack tips his hat and hollers in a booming voice, "Good evening, Guv-nuh. Welcome to New Providence."

After *The Vanity* passes, Rogers thinks back through all his experiences of many years at sea. Nothing like this has ever happened before. He quickly determines that the actions of the captain of the passing ship were planned carefully—a challenge of sorts. He knew exactly what he was doing. His goal was to mock Rogers' command, and in doing so, mock England herself. Rogers tells his quartermaster, "I want to know who that man is, the name of that ship, and the names of everyone aboard."

Chapter Sixteen

Passage To Nassau

Since James's plan to marry Anne and gain access to her future inheritance was shattered less than an hour after taking marriage vows, he reassesses his options. He understands that he must go back to what he knows best: working as a lowly deckhand aboard a merchant ship. Anne convinces James to use some of the money she has stolen from her father as a means for her to purchase passage on the ship Alyssa, the same ship that he has signed on to crew. The ship will be delivering goods to Nassau and then sailing on to Port Royal, Jamaica.

The more she spends time with James, the easier Anne finds it to manipulate him into thinking that all decisions they make are his. Her plan is working perfectly. Before paying for her passage, Anne tells James that she feels it would be easier for both of them if she were to use her maiden name aboard the ship, telling the captain that she plans to visit her wealthy uncle who owns a plantation on the interior of Nassau Island. This way, James can go about his work, as Anne enjoys the voyage through the cobalt blue Caribbean as a passenger aboard the vessel.

Sailing to Nassau, James busies himself with his duties as Anne walks the deck, talking to the captain and other men working the ship. Anne notices the sailors looking her over from head to toe each time she passes. Even the proper captain is caught numerous times appreciating the sight of Anne's voluptuous body—a rare sight on a ship at sea. She isn't the only one who notices the lustful looks. James sees them as well. He becomes agitated as his shipmates fill the foc'sle with talk of what they would do with the lovely Lady Cormac's body given half a chance. He continues the charade that they had contrived before the ship set sail—even pitching in his own lustful banter.

After asking many questions and participating in numerous conversations, Anne has learned more about life on the sea in two days than she has by reading hundreds of books and newspaper stories over the past three years. She also eavesdrops, listening in on the deckhands' private conversations, as they talk to each other in their own rough and explicit language.

This is only Anne's second voyage on a sailing ship. The first being when her father moved her and her mother to Charles Towne when she was far too young to remember many of the details of the experience. Yet now Anne is convinced that this is the life she wants to lead. However, tradition holds that a woman working aboard a ship at sea brings bad luck.

As the merchant ship approaches the port of New Providence, easing around the reef a half-mile offshore and exposing the full vista of the busy harbor, Anne notices two things—the brilliant blue-green waters and the many ships anchored there. Anne asks, "Captain, is it normal for so many ships to ride at anchor here?"

"Aye, my Lady. From a distance, you might conclude that New Providence is an incredibly busy port; however, the number of ships you see is deceiving, for many have been left to rot in this harbor. They are but derelicts."

"I don't understand."

"Well, you see, these waters and the township of New Providence are crowded with unsavory characters. It is known as a base for pirates planning their operations. These rogues abandon their ships, casting them aside when they become too worn and need too many repairs to maintain their seaworthiness. It's far easier—and I might guess a bit more of a challenge—for these sea dogs to take a new sloop when they need one."

"I see. But, you mentioned that these men take sloops. Why not take larger and more impressive ships like the man-o'-war that I have seen patrolling so often off the coast of Carolina? Are these men not ambitious?"

"The waters here are shallow and can be treacherous due

to the strong tides and rocky reefs. The hull of the smaller sloop doesn't drop as deeply and has less draft than the larger ships. While those are better suited for longer, open-water journeys, sloops are lighter, faster, and better suited for the pirates' ways. They can typically outpace most merchant and war ships, making it easier to get to their prizes or get away when outgunned."

The captain continued. "My dear lady, with the collection of rogues on this island, I'll admit to having a fair bit of fear for your wellbeing. I understand that you're here to visit your uncle in the interior of this isle. Is he meeting you when we arrive, or are you in need of a chaperone until he arrives for you? I would be happy to serve as your guardian until your meeting."

"Captain, thank you for your concern and your gracious offer to accompany me. However, I'll be fine until my uncle arrives."

Anne knows that the captain's intentions are noble, but she has also seen the way he looks at her. A young woman traveling alone presents an ideal opportunity for some playful shore leave spent on an overstuffed straw mattress.

CHAPTER SEVENTEEN

THE GOAT'S HEAD TAVERN

Anne leaves the ship and stays close by until James finishes his work and is paid. As they leave the docks and begin walking down the infamous Bay Street. Anne takes in the sights, having wondered since childhood if the reality would match the myth. She has grown up reading newspaper articles and hearing stories of how pirate crews, hard-drinking and hard-fighting mobs they were, fill the street with brawls, grog and loud dirges. Anne is disappointed. None of what she has heard appears to be at all accurate. A few rogues walk here and there, and one actually tips his hat to her as he passes. New Providence and Bay Street are not at all what she has expected.

James tells her, "Anne, before relieving the crew, the captain told us there have been dramatic changes as of late in New Providence. Just two weeks ago, the British arrived claiming this region as its own. The new guv-nuh has a mind—along with a king's commission—to abolish piracy in this region. He has given the pirates that called New Providence "home" two options: cease all acts of piracy at once and receive a full pardon, or continue on the account, be arrested, and ultimately hanged—having your carcass displayed on a pole at the entrance to the harbor as a warning for others.

"I reckon that if we'd landed here a month earlier, the landscape might have been much different. Most practicing pirates seem to have chosen not to test the British and accept the new guv-nuh's offer of a pardon. I'm sure that some holdouts remain. Still, this is not the best place for a lady to be. Keep close."

Anne still has some of the money that she stole from her father before leaving the Cormac estate. She and James rent a room at an inn next to a seedy-looking place called the Goat's Head Tavern. After they settle into their room, James and Anne spend the rest of the day making love—an art that Anne has yet to practice, much less master, James being her first. Based on what she has heard, other men simply must be better versed in the art than James is. She tells herself that his awkwardness and speedy finish are due to the fact that he has always paid women for his own pleasure and has, therefore, not been properly trained in the finer arts of satisfying a woman, particularly a woman with Anne's appetite for pleasure.

When evening comes, James and Anne venture out. At

night, Bay Street is a completely different world. The street is filled with all sorts of people. The sounds of men singing loudly, laughter, and the squeals of women fill Anne's ears. She inhales deeply and takes in a mixture of rich pipe smoke and the smell of food cooking. They step inside the Goat's Head Tavern. It is packed with men, and more than a few ladies of the evening—at least that is what she has heard them called, all surrounded by a haze of thick, dark smoke.

Anne leads the way to the bar. She thinks to herself, *this* is what she had expected New Providence to be. It is as if all the rogues who had taken the king's pardon have become nocturnal creatures who migrate to this place after the moon rises. Taking a broad, sweeping look around at the sights, Anne thinks to herself, *This is the place where I was meant to be.*

Her thought is interrupted as the barkeep abruptly barks out, "You, sir, what are you drinking this eve?"

Before James can respond, Anne turns to the bartender and says in a firm but polite way, "A bottle of rum and two glasses, please." Confused, James looks at the bartender as he raises one eyebrow and turns to fetch Anne's order. "Anne, don't get caught up in this moment."

The barkeep places the bottle and glasses in front of Anne. She pours, raises her glass and makes a toast. "James, to our future and this glorious place." He pauses just long enough to notice the sense of life and adventure that now fills her, and then hoists his glass alongside hers. The rum delivers a burning sensation as it washes down her throat. She winces and slams her glass down on the bar. James notices many of the men in the bar with their eyes firmly fixed on Anne. He quickly pours another shot, looks at her and at the men around the bar, and with quiet confidence, lifts his glass and says, "To my loving, beautiful, and faithful wife. May we live a long and happy life together!"

CHAPTER EIGHTEEN

TURNED INFORMANT

It's been said that good fortune quickly changes the perspective of those who allow setbacks to steer their emotions.

James and Anne decide to stay in New Providence until they find an opportunity for him to join on with a ship. Woodes Rogers, now officially installed as governor, has cracked down on piracy. He quickly makes examples of three pirates who have chosen to remain on the account rather than accept his pardon. They are tried for piracy and executed by hanging, sending a clear message that the new governor is deadly serious. Piracy is now an enterprise in decline and being continued only in secrecy. The few jack-tars who have chosen to remain with the pirate brotherhood—perhaps under the influence of far too much cheap rum—have left New Providence to find new waters in which to operate. The ships and crews that have decided to continue are not left wanting for additional deckhands.

The remaining pirates are fearful that Rogers will infiltrate their ships by placing hired informants among them. Such men are selected personally by Rogers to seek the names of the captains and their crews in order that they are found and brought to justice as quickly and efficiently as possible. As soon as Rogers is settled, he instructs his men to spread the word that good money will be paid to those who provide the information he seeks. There are no friends among thieves.

Three months pass and the money that James has made working as a deckhand aboard the merchant ship, together with the money that Anne took from her father, is quickly running out. Each time a ship drops anchor for a day or two in any decent-sized harbor or settlement, James tries his hand at manual labor. As he has done many times in the past, he realizes that hard work does not suit him well. However, to convince Anne that he has the capacity to provide for her, he chooses to take easy money by becoming an informant for Rogers.

In New Providence for a day, James finds his way to the old Spanish fort that Rogers has quite lavishly converted into his home and the official seat of government. James links his fate and fortune to the will of the region's new viceroy. Situated atop a high hill overlooking the port, it provides an ideal vantage point for spotting ships entering the harbor. The fort had been abandoned by the Spanish years earlier as they left Nassau. Rogers employs many of the former pirates in making the repairs needed to make the fort a worthy governor's residence. Announcing his intentions to become an informant to the British troops manning the guardhouse at the front gate, James is granted an appointment to meet with the governor.

Two days later, at the appointed time, James returns to the governor's headquarters and is led into Rogers' office. The door is opened, and James enters the room, hoping that his broad stride might hide his timidity. Without rising from his desk, Rogers gives his visitor a quick glance before asking, "Well, now, what might your name be?" James lets out a nervous cough and replies, "My name be James Bonny, sir." James hears someone behind him. He turns to see Morris Cooper smiling at him.

Rogers pauses, recognizing the name. "Ah. Mister Bonny, I hear that you are in a position to provide my office with quite a few names of those who continue to break the laws enacted by the British Crown. Is this correct?"

James hesitates. "Yes, I am your guv-nuhship."

"Good. The information you provide must be accurate. I will pay three quid for each captain's name, two quid for five shipmates and two quid for divulging any plans these sea dogs have for plying their ill-thought trade in this region. Mister Bonny, are these terms acceptable to you?"

James hesitates again—longer this time—realizing that the knowledge he has just become a valuable asset. "Yes, they are your guv-nuhship."

"Excellent. As you are now in the loyal service of King George, Mister Cooper here will have you sign papers to this effect as you leave. I look forward to a mutually profitable relationship, as do you, I'm sure," Woodes says, this time standing to indicate the end of the appointment. "Good day, Mister Bonny."

"Thank you, guv-nuh, and good day to you."

Rogers walks toward his large bay window facing the ocean and sees James leaving the compound as the guard opens the gate. He says, "Cooper, although we encourage these men to take pay for the information we seek, I despise them for accepting our offer. In private, I will tell you that paid informants are the lowest of the low—bilge rats. They have no integrity, no honor. They are spineless creatures who will sell out their own kind for little money." Cooper walks over to stand next to Rogers at the window. The king's new man in Providence continues.

"When recruiting these scalawags by speaking face-to-face, I tell them that I honor them for becoming an ally of the British Crown and for doing the right thing. I tell them that only brave souls and men with conviction are willing to provide us with the information we need. This bloody charade eats at my very being."

Rogers continues to look out his window, and he notices three former pirates who accepted his offer of clemency mending an interior stone wall on the property. At first glance, he believes that they are making good on their promise to earn an honest day's pay. As he looks closer, he realizes that they only appear to be working. One of the men looks around and thinking that the coast is clear, reaches into a bag and pulls out a bottle of liquor. He draws a big swig and passes the bottle to his former shipmate. Rogers then looks at the third man who is now leaning against a tree falling asleep.

Rogers thinks to himself, *"These 'reformed' pirates, they've grown to become a lazy lot and cannot even manage to muster an honest day's work. I should have them flogged."* He turns from his window, stumbles awkwardly and nearly falls. He quickly catches himself by grabbing the corner of his desk and regaining his balance.

Cooper takes a step toward Rogers, "Governor—do you need assistance, sir?"

"I am fine. It's my bad foot, a souvenir I brought back from one of my expeditions. The same expedition that also left me with this." Rogers points to his badly scarred face and props himself up as he sits on the corner of his desk.

Cooper summons his courage. "I had heard that you received your wounds during a great battle when you were victorious over the Spaniards and captured the *Disengaño*. I would consider it an honor if you were to give me a firsthand account of events that took place during your expedition— that is, if you feel up to it, sir."

Rogers paused, stared up at the ceiling and then directly into his officer's eyes. "Aye Cooper, I received these wounds at that time, during my first expedition as captain. My memories are as clear as if the battle took place a month ago. During the winter of 1708, we were having very little luck finding ships to take when sailing the eastern coast of South America. Over a four-month span, we had taken only two small sloops, lightly laden. Searching for more profitable waters, we made our way south in the direction of Patagonia."

"Towards the cape?" Cooper asked, astonished. "I've heard the stories ..."

Cutting him off, Rogers speaks loudly, closing his eyelids as if to relive the memory in the moment. "Aye! As we approached the cape, a tremendous storm fell upon us—the seas were unforgiving. We drove into sustained winds of 50 to 70 knots—and only 10 or 15 points off the bow. Some gusts reached up to 85, and waves broke over the ship reaching the top of the foremast, I tell you. All we did not have a chance to secure was swept from our decks and into the sea, including four of my men."

Rogers continues, "And 'twerent just the wind and water, mate. We believed that if the storm did not sink us, we would surely freeze to death. Ice encrusted everything above the waterline, adding tons of weight."

Cooper stands mesmerized by the story. "But sir, you could've capsized."

Rogers cut him off. "And we nearly did a dozen times, heeling over 30 to 40 degrees and causing the terrified crew to climb the deck by whatever means to the windward side praying in terror the entire time."

"The storm began late afternoon and raged on through the night. The winds were so powerful that we could not hold our course. After the storm subsided, we realized how far off course we had been pushed. Based on our calculations—as ye know, there are few navigational stars yet known that far south beside the Southern Cross and with a sky covered in clouds, we had no chance of taking a noon sun sight. So, we figured that we were farther south than any humans had ever been.

"We soon corrected our course and headed due north, leaving Tierra del Fuego on our starboard stern and moving on a broad reach up the western coast of South America. The combination of the torturous weather and our lack of success finding prizes discouraged my crew. I soon began hearing frequent arguments taking place amongst them. My officers informed me that some members of the company had been speaking mutiny. I realized something had to change soon, or my officers and I would likely face trouble—with but two possible outcomes. Either we would fight and suppress the mutiny, allied with shipmates loyal to my command, or I would lose my command and be marooned to die, along with any remaining officers loyal to me."

Cooper adds, "And that region is certainly no Eden in which to be marooned."

"Aye," Rogers says. "And we knew it. It's been said that good fortune quickly changes the perspective of those who allow setbacks to steer their emotions. In our case, our good fortune began to change after we rescued a marooned seaman named Alexander Selkirk off the coast of Chile. Bringing Selkirk aboard with us changed everything.

"Since we could not find suitable prizes on water, I devised plans to try our luck on land. In April 1709, after laying in a healthy supply of fresh water and gargantuan tortoises at what the Spaniards call the Galapagos, we sailed due east and laid siege to the Ecuadorian town of Guayaquil. We sent an envoy to discuss our terms with the town's leaders. They were informed that if a ransom of 30,000 pieces of eight were not paid by the time the sun reached its apex the next day, we would attack and plunder the town. Eighteen hours later, the town delivered a ransom of 22,000 pieces of eight."

"Why did they only pay you 22,000 pieces of eight and not the 30,000 you demanded?"

"We did not feel inclined to ask them why. Since they did not pay us the full ransom we demanded, we snuck ashore after sailing out of the harbor that afternoon and into a tiny inlet only a short march away, and sacked the town at midnight under the cover of darkness and stripped it of everything worth taking—from its homes, its businesses, and its inhabitants.

Then we sailed west, from whence we came, into the vastness of the Pacific, to avoid any Spanish pursuers. We anchored our ships in a pristine cove on the lee side of a large island in the Galapagos, perfectly on the equator—zero degrees both north and south my good man. While resting on these islands, we carefully planned our next action. The success of our raid on Guayaquil set us on a course for the most active and lucrative phase of the whole expedition. And before it was all over, we had captured and plundered twenty ships."

"When I had first heard these numbers, I immediately knew you to be a brave and noble commander, sir," said Cooper.

"During our Galapagos sojourn, William Dampier, my sail master on the *Duchess*, informed me that when he sailed on a previous expedition thirteen years earlier he recalled hearing of a Spanish ship called the Manila Galleon. This treasure ship made an annual trip from the Philippines to Acapulco, a thousand leagues due north of Guayaquil laden with a cargo of gold and fine porcelain. Once safely in Acapulco, the cargo was transported overland to Vera Cruz, where it was then shipped across the Atlantic to Spain. The treasure that these ships carried was described as unimaginable in magnitude—dozens of cargoes—joining together from all of Central America. Dampier knew both the course and the timeframe in which the Manila ship would sail.

Although this information came to him many years earlier, I believed that his information was sound and charted our course. Dampier said the ship would arrive during November and December, off the southernmost point of the Baja Peninsula, near a place called Fines Terre, before heading across the Sea of Cortez to Acapulco.

"We made our way to the Baja Peninsula to await the Manila Galleon. Our ships rendezvoused in October and spent seven weeks cruising off the coast—waiting. I considered at some point over the years that Manila treasure ship had altered its course or changed its schedule to take advantage of the Humboldt Current and trade winds more fully, or that Dampier's information was simply not reliable. Regardless, we had waited long enough. It was time to move on."

Rogers continues as Cooper walks casually to the window, still enraptured with the tale. "On the thirty-first day of December, I reluctantly made the decision to set sail for Asia. On the first day of January 1710, we made our final preparations for the long voyage across the Pacific. Only hours before, we were to set sail, a lookout shouted out with excitement from his perch atop the foremast. He had sighted the *Disengaño*. The Spanish spotted us on a course to intercept them and turned about in an attempt to bide time and prepare for battle.

"Knowing the galleon was a merchantman, I naturally assumed her to be poorly armed, and there was no escort. As we closed the distance, I noticed the size of the *Disengaño*. She was large and did carry 20 large guns and 193 men. When we finally overtook her, we engaged in a running battle, with heavy iron smashing masts and shredding canvas.

"During the fight, a musket ball pierced my left cheek and shattered much of my upper jaw. The impact knocked me senseless and the last thing I remembered before losing consciousness was the sight of four of my bloodied teeth hitting the deck.

Rogers paused, breathing deeply several times before continuing. "When I regained my faculties, I came to face down in a pool of my blood. I looked up to see the deck of my ship in utter chaos. The *Duke* and *Disengaño* were now bound together in a web of ropes and grappling hooks, and boarding parties from each covered both decks. The fighting aboard both ships was fierce, with cannon shot firing at point-blank range and snipers taking aim at officers and cannoneers from the shrouds. The Spaniards were determined not to relinquish their treasure and we were determined to take it."

Rogers pauses again, bracing himself with his hands upon the large desk and lowers his gaze to the floor. "It was at this time that I saw my younger brother take a musket ball to his side. As he fell, he was run through by a cutlass. He was dead before he fell to the deck. "

The room is silent for several long moments before Rogers continues. Cooper, not knowing the appropriate reaction, stands motionless at the window, his head also lowered.

"The battle lasted for three long and arduous hours before we finally gained the upper hand. Not a moment too soon, our other ships, the *Duchess* and *Marquis,* joined in the battle, engaging the Spaniard's from the opposite side of their ship. I did not know that in addition to my jaw being shattered, a large fragment of the musket ball had lodged itself in the roof of my mouth. I continued my command throughout the battle, but was forced to write orders or use crude hand motions, due to the pain and blood loss I suffered in attempting to speak.

"When the battle was over late in the afternoon, we had slain nine Spaniards and wounded ten. Only two of my crew had been killed and six wounded."

Cooper leans against the large window frame, motionless, staring intently. He breaks his silence with a question. "Governor, did you find the incredible wealth that Dampier said would be onboard the galleon?"

"Aye Cooper, we sailed the *Disengaño* back to Saint Lucas to unload our prisoners and search the ship. Searching the cargo, we found gold, gems, spices, porcelain, and silks worth more than £150,000—quite literally a king's ransom. All aboard rejoiced except for me. I could not stop thinking that my brother was now dead—already slipped over the ship's side from a galley table, a cannonball chained to his ankles, to take his place in Davey Jones' locker. The image as I held him in my arms still haunts me today.

"Dampier reminded me that a second galleon should soon be on the horizon. We confirmed the existence of a second ship by torturing five prisoners. We learned that there was indeed a second galleon sailing the same course, only a day behind the *Disengaño*. It was an even larger and heavier ship, carrying perhaps twice the cargo, by the name of *Nuestra Señora de Begoña*. The *Begoña* was a massive 750-ton ship embarking 450 crewmen. Its battery of 30 twelve-pound guns was twice the size of our complement.

The *Duchess* and the *Marquis* first sighted and attacked the *Begoña* on the fourth day of January. The battle raged for three days. Despite my wound, I ordered the *Duke* to make sail and catch up to join the fight, and finally doing so on the second day of the battle. We estimated that between our three ships, at least five hundred shots struck the enemy without piercing its hull. The toughness of their ship's hull was matched only by the toughness of its crew, which resisted us fiercely.

The Spanish were resolved to defend their vessel and its treasure to the end. The *Begoña's* defenders dropped firebombs onto our lower vessels. One of these bombs exploded in the magazine of my ship, sending wooden splinters and iron shrapnel though the air and ripping a two-and-a-half-inch notch from my heel. Even though I was in considerable pain, I continued to command our attack. I would not give up until we captured the prize.

After days of fighting, the much larger and heavily armed galleon had pounded our three ships into little more than smashed hulks. All were heavily damaged. Thirty of my men were killed, and eighteen were wounded. It was in our best interest to break off our attack before the *Begoña* sent one or all of us to the bottom. I wanted that ship more than life itself. So, we all exerted our last and hardest efforts, finally causing the enemy to lower its flag.

After the battle, we renamed the *Disengaño* the *Bachelor* and added it to our flotilla. Repairs were made to our battered ships, and we returned to England where we sold our captured ships and the wealth of treasures we had gained from our expedition."

Cooper smiles contently and replies, "What an incredible journey you have lived at sea. With all that you have been through, do you miss the life aboard a ship?"

"No Cooper, that was a different time in my life, one that I gladly set aside for this post. I was tormented by what I experienced during my longest expedition but over time I have been able to reconcile with the demons that haunted me." Rogers once again looks out his window and says, "I recall the weather being similar to today, gray sky and still."

As James heads back to the Goat's Head Tavern, he already feels guilty, knowing that the information he will provide the British could very well lead to the death of men he has befriended. He also knows that he does not dare tell Anne he is spying on the people they have both grown to know these past three months. Anne would never forgive him. However, over the following weeks, Anne notices a difference in James. As they make their nightly stop at the Goat's Head Tavern, she sees his personality shift from being awkwardly quiet to outgoing. He uncharacteristically begins to strike-up casual conversation with most in the tavern, asking many questions.

Anne says, "James, I've noticed that you've become chatty with all sorts, some of whom you've never talked to before."

"Chatty? Damn it, Anne, can't a man talk to whoever he

wants without having a woman count the number of words leaving his mouth?"

This defensive response tells Anne that something is not right. James is keeping something from her. She also notices that they should have run out of money more than a week earlier, but now James seems to have plenty for their needs.

A month passes, and James is rarely home with Anne. She is left mostly to herself. Predictably, without the daily connection needed to keep any strong romance alive, she and James quickly drift apart. Showing up at the inn late one night, Anne catches the whiff of a strong combination of rum and perfume. Later, he joins Anne in bed and begins making the gentle overtures that always let Anne know satisfying his manly needs is foremost on his mind. Anne, the high-spirited soul that she is, lets it quickly be known that she wants no part of this. Planting a foot squarely against his chest she heaves her frisky mate out of bed and onto the floor where he lands with a loud thud. He will spend the rest of the night there.

A full bucket of cold water greets the slumbering James the following morning. Wiping his face, he stares up to see the fiery Anne, standing fully dressed with legs apart in a stiff stance and hands braced solidly on her hips. The empty bucket has hit the floor within inches of his head.

Still shaking off the chill of such a rude awakening, James peers up and asks, somewhat meekly, "My Anne—what in the bloody hell did you do that for?"

As Anne prepares to speak, James quickly realizes the mistake of asking such an open-ended question. "For starters, it's to wash away the stink of whatever whore enjoyed your company last night." James places his hands over his eyes, blocking out the light. Anne continues.

"To let you know I'm not pleased in the least with your conduct here almost since the day we arrived. Is it the lure of new and luscious women that keeps you away most of the time? What exactly are you doing to earn us the income we so desperately need? I need answers, James, and I want them now."

James slowly lifts his head and shakes the water droplets from his hair. Peering up at Anne, he speaks softly, as if the walls themselves had ears. "For income, my dear Anne, I'm working for important men who seek my knowledge!"

"Ha, what knowledge could you possibly possess that would be worth anything to these *important men* of yours — your opinion of the finest rum or the best whore to bed with?"

"No, Anne. I'm working for the governor himself. He pays me well to listen to conversations at taverns and the docks. I listen and then report back what I hear."

"So you've lowered yourself from being a seafaring man of the world to becoming a bloody spy ... *and* bedding with whores."

"Yes, Anne, if you must know, you're right on both counts. There is much to learn from ladies who share their beds with other men of import."

Anne paused for a minute, deciding for herself that James' excuse was as likely to be true as false. Then she spoke quite firmly, looking down upon James with disdain. "James, you are the lowest of the low, and I want nothing to do with you. I care not to see your face again. Get out now."

Chapter Nineteen

Chidley Bayard

Still fuming from her earlier argument with James, Anne takes a walk to collect her thoughts. As she walks toward the market, she passes a large merchant ship tied up at the main cargo dock, its contents being unloaded by a dozen strong-backed men. Anne looks at the ship and notices a sharply dressed, handsome man. He stands on the gangway asking a deckhand for an accounting of goods that have just been unloaded from his ship.

As he talks, Anne notices that she catches his eye. Anne serves up a grin as she passes the ship. The man, distracted only for a moment, redirects his attention from Anne back to the business at hand. A half-hour later, Anne is buying fresh oranges from an old woman with a fruit cart in the open-air market. As she places the oranges in Anne's wooden basket, Anne looks beyond the woman and sees the same well-dressed man she passed earlier at the docks. He is acting as if he is also planning to purchase fruit. The man sees Anne looking at him, smiles, and walks over to engage her.

"My lady, may I take the liberty to introduce myself?"

Anny replies coyly, "Why yes, you may."

"My name is Chidley Bayard," says the man as he doffs his hat in the customary fashion. "And to whom might I have the pleasure of speaking with this fine day?"

"My name is Anne Bonny, Mister Bayard, and I have a question for you: when visiting New Providence do you often make it a habit to seek fresh fruit, or is your intention today to seek fresh conversation?"

"I beg your pardon, Madame. I would be lying if I were to tell you that I frequent this market for fresh fruit. I saw you pass my ship earlier, and I was compelled to know your name."

"Mister Bayard, it looks as though you've accomplished much today. You've found fresh fruit, and you now know my name. What are you compelled to do next?"

Chidley smiles and replies, "Well, my dear lady, I know that this seems spectacularly forward of me, knowing that we've only just been introduced, but I find myself compelled to ask you to join me for dinner this evening at my estate. I plan to be on the island for but a short time and you would do me a great honor if you would join me this evening."

Anne is intrigued by both Bayard's refined looks and his masterful use of the English language. Perhaps most of all, she is intrigued by his playful and forward conversation and manner. With James's adultery fresh on her mind, along with the fact that he may as well be gone from her life, Anne agrees to dine with Bayard. "Mister Bayard, I will be delighted to be your guest this evening."

"Excellent! Where might I send my carriage to fetch you?"

"I shall be in front of your ship promptly at six."

"And so it shall be." Bayard politely takes Anne's free hand and leaves a gentle kiss on her soft, cotton glove. "Until then."

CHAPTER TWENTY

DINNER FOR TWO

Anne wears her finest dress and leaves the Goat's Head Tavern to wait for Chidley Bayard's carriage to arrive. His black coach, drawn by two snow-white horses, arrives for her at exactly six o'clock. Anne marvels at the impressive carriage as the equally impressive coachman greets her and opens the carriage door helping her in. The coach travels for nearly forty minutes to the interior of the island. It finally arrives at a long cinder drive lined with trees that create a canopy of intertwined branches and leaves. As the carriage approaches, Anne is amazed at the grandeur of Bayard's home. The mansion is an enormous English-style manor sitting on a thousand acres of land. Anne whispers to herself, *Who in God's name is this man?*

Anne exits the coach and is greeted by a house servant, "My lady, Welcome to the Bayard estate. If you will, please follow me. Lord Bayard has been looking forward to your arrival and is waiting in the main dining room."

Anne follows the polite gray-haired servant through a long hallway to the opposite end of the home, where the dining room is situated. She marvels at the lavish decor. Growing up in Charles Towne, Anne has led a life of privilege. She has known wealth all of her life before coming to New Providence. However, the wealth she has known pales in comparison to what she sees around her. The house servant opens the large wooden doors to the dining room. Seated at the far end of an enormous dining table decorated with the finest silver, linen and china, Chidley stands and greets her. "Lady Bonny, you look absolutely exquisite. Welcome to my home. I hope that your journey from the port was not too hard on you. The roads leading to the interior of the isle are not as refined as those near the coast."

"Thank you. The journey was not too difficult."

"I had Thomas prepare a more comfortable setting for our dining this evening. This table is better suited for larger gatherings. Come with me."

Chidley leads Anne out to his courtyard, where a small round candlelit table is waiting for them. During dinner, Chidley learns more about Anne, her background, and how she ended up in New Providence. Most of what she tells him about how she managed to find herself in New Providence is a story that she has made up on the spot. She does not tell him that she is married to a lazy adulterer who betrays all he knows as an informant for the British, or that she cavorts with rogues nightly at the Goat's Head Tavern. Instead, she conjures a tale and tells him that she comes from a wealthy family in Charles Towne, Carolina. She says that she has found her way to Nassau to visit a friend, sailing to the island on a merchant ship under contract to one of her father's business associates.

Anne asks Chidley how he established his residence on Nassau. Chidley tells her, "I was raised in Hertford, England, a small town north of London. I attended Oxford, and upon my graduation, I took the road less traveled. Hearing about the vast opportunity for trade in the New World, I purchased a modest vessel and began importing consumable goods from England and other European countries to Jamaica. I expanded my operations to Cuba, Hispaniola, and New Providence. I have been doing so for years and have created a fleet of ships that sail the Atlantic. I've been blessed with great fortune."

During dinner the two talk comfortably, laugh, and consume three bottles of wine. After dinner, they move from the courtyard to Chidley's study, where they drink the finest port from Europe. Shortly thereafter, Anne finds herself in Chidley's bedroom.

Chidley faces Anne, takes her hands and tells her, "Anne, I've led a life of conservatism. I've worked hard and have earned much wealth. My disciplined upbringing, my focus on studies, and my business dealings have made the years pass quickly. Life has not afforded me the opportunity to live as others do. I have known few women. Today, as I saw you walking near my ship, I knew that I had to know your name. I hoped that you would find your way to me."

Chidley kisses Anne softly on her neck, then her cheek and her lips. The heavy mixture of alcohol and passion drives them to a frenzied state as they pull and tug at each other's clothes, stripping down to nothing. As they fall into Chidley's bed, Anne launches a passionately aggressive attack on him.

Chidley abruptly pulls Anne's arms away from him, pinning them, and her, to his bed and says, "No, Anne, not this way."

Anne stops her assault and with a confused voice says, "I don't understand."

"Anne, let me show you." He releases her arms and begins slowly to caress her body as he kisses her. They make love for hours before falling asleep. The next morning, Anne wakes with an alcohol-induced headache. She realizes that she is alone in Chidley's bed. She sees a note and a single red rose next to her. The note reads, *Anne, I look at our meeting as nothing more than fate. It would give me great pleasure if you were to dine with me again this evening. Chidley.*

CHAPTER TWENTY-ONE

LOST AND FOUND

Anne's relationship with Chidley grows. They dine and sleep together every night for two weeks. Chidley begins buying Anne expensive jewelry and gives her money to go into town to buy what she pleases. One night while dining, Chidley tells Anne that he has planned a large gala at his estate before he leaves Nassau for business in England. Chidley plans five lavish parties a year at his estate in order to build and maintain his social status. He invites only aristocrats, influential business owners, and government officials. This event will entertain over one-hundred-twenty people. Some will travel from as far as Cuba, Hispaniola, and Jamaica. Anne revels in the opportunity to be introduced as Chidley's companion.

As guests arrive the evening of the gala, Bayard's house servant, Thomas, announces them as they enter the large ballroom. Chidley walks around the room to greet each guest personally, and he introduces Anne as "Lady Anne Bonny." As the mingling intensifies, Chidley engages his influential guests in light conversation that helps reinforce his status as the dominant merchant trader and one of the richest men in the Caribbean. These conversations appear to be innocent in nature but are all well planned, each having a specific purpose. Chidley's conversations will be continued and expanded upon days after the party.

When Chidley begins talking business, Anne knows that it is improper for a lady to listen. She politely excuses herself and wanders through the ballroom. Earlier in the evening, Chidley had introduced Anne to Elizabeth Lawes, the sister-in-law of Governor Nicholas Lawes of Jamaica. While Chidley continues his conversations, Anne strikes up a conversation with Elizabeth. Anne is not aware that Elizabeth, and a few other ladies attending the gala, heard rumors that Anne has purposely sought out Chidley for his money and is sleeping with him in order to gain access to his fortune. Elizabeth is a woman of good standing, and the thought of Anne using her body to manipulate him is incomprehensible to her. Elizabeth sees Anne walking toward her across the dance floor. She could easily have acted as if she does not see her and simply turned in the opposite direction, but Elizabeth chooses to stand her ground. Anne, not knowing what Elizabeth thinks of her, attempts to begin a conversation.

"Elizabeth, did you travel from Jamaica to attend

Chidley's gala this evening?"

Elizabeth stares forward and does not respond. Since Elizabeth does not respond, Anne assumes that she simply did not hear her due to the echoing sound of the music and conversations taking place around them.

Anne repeats her question louder. "Elizabeth, forgive me, with all the music and laughter, I am sure that it's difficult to hear me. I asked you if you traveled from Jamaica to attend Chidley's gala this evening."

Meanwhile, Chidley, still engaged in a conversation, sees Anne from across the ballroom talking to Elizabeth and smiles. As he talks, he continues to watch Anne and he marvels at her beauty and grace.

After Anne repeats her question, Elizabeth continues to stare straight ahead and begins to wave her fan in front of her face. Anne realizes that Elizabeth has indeed heard her but is purposely ignoring her. This causes Anne's blood to boil. Chidley has known Anne for only a short while and does not know how her temper can turn in a heartbeat when provoked. He continues to watch Anne from across the room, thinking that she and Elizabeth are engaged in polite conversation. Anne does not like how this pompous woman is treating her and walks directly in front of her so that they are face-to-face. Elizabeth has no choice but to look Anne in the eye and, while doing so, rolls her eyes in disgust.

Anne stares intently at Elizabeth and says, "Well, my good lady, it appears that you are not deaf and can hear me.

Why do you have no tongue to answer me?"

"Madame, I did hear you, and I don't make it a habit to speak with sorts such as yourself."

"Sorts such as myself?"

"Yes, everyone but Chidley knows what you're doing, using your cunning and your body as tools to gain his trust and access his fortune. Why don't you leave and go back from where you came? I cannot allow you to continue with your charade. I plan to tell Chidley that which I and everyone else suspect your intentions to be. So kindly put distance between us now."

Anne replies, "Kindly put distance between us, distance?"

Anne's face turns beet-red, her nose wrinkles, and she begins to lose control. Elizabeth does not know the fury she has just ignited. Elizabeth smirks at Anne. This reaction enrages Anne and pushes her beyond her limits. In a swift motion, Anne rears back and punches Elizabeth squarely in the mouth. The force of the punch causes Elizabeth to take two unbalanced steps backward before losing her footing and landing flat on her back, prostrate on the dance floor.

Chidley cannot believe what he has just seen and yells, "Anne!" He quickly makes his way across the ballroom toward her and the fallen Elizabeth. Everyone in close proximity to the two women freezes and stares with shock as Elizabeth puts her hand to her mouth and realizes that her two front teeth have just been knocked free from her head. She rolls from her sitting position onto her knees and starts crawling on the dance floor, desperately searching for her teeth.

With her fists still tightly clenched, Anne wears a satisfied, smile on her face. She stands over Elizabeth and attentively watches as she continues to look frantically for her two front teeth. All the while, blood drips from her mouth and her tall white wig hangs off-kilter from her head. Anne says, "Elizabeth, you look completely different from this perspective." She spots one of Elizabeth's teeth on the floor, pushes it with her foot toward Elizabeth and mocks, "Here you go, love—lost and found."

Chidley races toward Anne, grabs her by her shoulders, looks at her and questions, "Anne, why?"

As the governor's sister-in-law is attended to, Chidley motions for his servants. He tells them to see Anne to his room and not let her out until he comes for her. He then looks to the band positioned on the loft overlooking the ballroom and motions for them to continue playing, hoping to distract his guests from the catastrophe.

Minutes later, Chidley storms up the stairs to his room. The servants step aside and he tells them, "Stay where you are." He jerks the door open and slams it behind him. He is enraged by what Anne has just done. "Obviously, I misunderstood you to be a lady, when, indeed, you are nothing more than a common vagrant I found wandering the streets of New Providence. I cannot afford for your actions to destroy all that I've worked so hard for. Your behavior is incomprehensible, and the damage you have caused me may be irreversible. Anne, as of this moment, you and I never existed."

Chidley opens the doors to his room and tells his servants, "Escort this woman out of my home, and have my carriage drop her off at the New Providence docks where I found her."

Shortly thereafter, Anne finds herself stepping out of Bayard's carriage just yards from the Goat's Head Tavern. Anne enters the tavern to see James sitting at a table in a darkened corner, drinking alone. No one associates with him, after learning that he has turned informant for Woodes Rogers. Those who do speak to him only talk to him to feed him stories that they have made up, knowing that he will report their misinformation to the governor's office.

Anne looks at James and thinks, *What a pitiful sight!*" As she approaches, he says, "Anne, you're a sight for my sore eyes." The two talk and reconcile, agreeing that they will stay true to each other and that James will not continue his work as an informant.

CHAPTER TWENTY-TWO

THE DUTCH PRIZE

The Vanity has been at sea for months. They have been raiding merchant ships at will, up and down the colonial coast. Their hull is full of stolen provisions—gold, silver, and other items of value. Jack paces the deck and hears the shipmate perched high above him as a lookout, "Ship ahoy, off starboard bow!"

He opens his spyglass and peers into the distance scanning the horizon. The sun is setting quickly behind the ship, turning it into a darkened silhouette, but he sees Dutch colors. "Men, it looks like the Dutch have been kind enough to send us another prize. Quartermaster, set a course to engage it and raise our flag."

Jack is particularly proud of his flag. Many pirate ships use the traditional white skull and crossbones on a black background. The most notorious captains create their own unique flag designs to distinguish themselves from others.

Jack recalls seeing the flag of Edward Teach, known by most citizens as "Blackbeard." Teach's flag captivated his imagination. It was completely unique and terrifying. Teach's flag incorporated a full-bodied skeleton with devil horns atop its head, raising a goblet in one hand and a lance stabbing a disembodied red heart in the other. When the crew voted Jack its captain, he designed his flag using a traditional white skull, but instead of the common crossbones, he chose two crossed sabers. He told his crew, "Lads, by using sabers 'stead of bones will show the poor souls we happen upon at sea. The sight of the flag alone will intimidate captains and their crews. I wager that the sight of our flag will make many tremble with fear and surrender without a fight."

The Dutch captain sees the ship turn in their direction and hears one of his men call out, "Zij zijn piraten!" ("They are pirates!") The Dutch captain knows that his ship is loaded heavily with cargo from Europe and is larger and slower than the sloop headed toward them. His only chance is to turn his ship west to capture the strong trade winds in its sails. He knows he cannot outrun his pursuer, but his ship may be able to maintain its distance for a while in order to buy time. His hope is that they will cross paths with a friendly ship to support them before the pursuing pirates close their distance and launch an attack.

Jack uses his spyglass to see what action the Dutch captain will take. He knows that after seeing a pirate's flag, some captains surrender their vessels without a fight. The fear is that the raiders will attack without mercy, steal their cargo, their ships, and their lives. If they give up without a fight, pirates are often more merciful to their prisoners. Jack sees that the Dutch ship has turned in the opposite direction. He drops his spyglass from his eye, and his quartermaster says, "Captain Rackham, what are your orders?" Still looking intently in the direction of the fleeing ship, Jack lets out a sarcastic chuckle. "Stay on our present course. Why do the Dutch always try to make a run of it? With this stiff wind behind our backs, we will close the distance on her soon enough. Have the crew prepare for battle. Tell the master gunner to load our cannons and ready them to fire. Oh ... and quartermaster, have the 'feared and large dark one' beat on the large drum we took from the Spaniards last week. The lads will like the drama the beat will add to this adventure."

The Vanity gains on the Dutch ship. As the Dutch captain realizes trying to outrun his ship's pursuer is futile, he orders his navigator to turn hard so that his ship will position its guns broadside toward the approaching ship.

Jack yells to his men, "Mates, it looks like there will be a battle this evening." The sun almost completely disappears from the horizon, and only a light glow remains, reflecting off the ocean's surface. The ships align parallel to each other to square off. The Dutch ship fires first. Plumes of smoke and flashes of fire are seen before the booming of its cannons is heard. The Dutch shots fall short of *The Vanity* and splash harmlessly in the water several hundred yards away. "Lads, the inexperienced Dutch boy shot too soon and has just shown us his hand. Their guns are lighter than ours. We will stay out of their range and pound them for a bit from a distance before boarding."

As *The Vanity* edges slightly closer, Jack tells the quartermaster, "Knock the mast off that damned ship ... fire all guns. We will teach them to run from us."

"Aye, aye, captain!" The quartermaster relays the order to the Master Gunner, who in turn, yells out the orders to the ships gun crew. The fuse of each cannon is ignited one after the other. The first volley falls slightly short of the ship. The gunners use their first shots to adjust their trajectory and hone in on their target. The second salvo slams hard into the Dutch ship, exploding a portion of its deck. Shards of wood splinters and iron shrapnel fly in all directions and slice through the deckhands' bodies.

Three shots hit the ship broadside, rocking her violently in the water, causing the entire structure to shudder. The accuracy of *The Vanity*'s barrage is too much for the merchant ship, and it quickly raises a white flag to signal its surrender. The battle is over in a matter of minutes.

Jack, surprised by their quick surrender, yells, "They've had enough. Steer us around the backside just in case of trickery." The crew uses its grappling hooks to latch onto the listing ship, pulling the two ships side-by-side. As Jack and his crew board the vessel, he surveys the length of the ship to assess the damage. He sees a number of the Dutch crew sitting on the deck, with their hands raised over their heads, as small fires burn around them.

Several of the Dutch lie dead on the deck. The light cast from the full moon and the small blazes reflect off pools of blood. The ship is completely silent.

Jack whispers, "Easy, men. Be on your guard. Something's not right." At this moment, six men suddenly appear from behind a blind spot on the deck and fire their muskets. The men who appeared to have surrendered, along with several more who were playing dead, spring to their feet, firing pistols and wielding their swords. The surprise fire hits four of Jack's men, who immediately fall. Jack yells, "Take them, lads!" As his men storm toward their attackers, they scream at the top of their lungs while firing their weapons. A shipmate lofts a grenade at the six riflemen reloading their guns as they take cover behind the wooden structure. One of the riflemen sees the light from the fuse as it hits the deck and bounces toward him and his shipmates. He drops his weapon, quickly grabs the grenade and raises his arm to throw it back at *The Vanity*. His arm flies forward, releasing the bomb, but the fuse reaches its end and explodes only inches from the man's hand, instantly disintegrating his hand and a portion of his forearm and showering the others with exploding iron pellets. Four of the six fall dead on the spot, while the other two lie on the deck mortally wounded. Jack sees a blurred image of a man streak past him. He turns to see Ajani raising his sword over his head with both arms. With full force, he slams his cutlass down on top of a Dutch crewmember's head as he kneels to reload his weapon.

The force of the blow cleaves the Dutch sailor's head

cleanly in half. Severed arteries spray blood across Ajani's face, and upper torso. Jack freezes for a split second in awe of the devastating act of violence just witnessed. Ajani, not fazed, pulls his sword free from the dead man's body and continues on to engage another Dutch sailor. Chaos mixes with pure adrenaline, and the fight rages for thirty minutes as Jack's crew overpowers the Dutch.

All of the noises of battle begin to subside. Only a handful of the Dutch crew survives to surrender. They are shuffled aboard *The Vanity,* as they are taken prisoner. As Jack begins to leave the ship, he hears the sound of clinking swords coming from the far aft side of the vessel. As he turns the corner, he sees a gathering of his men watching two of their mates engage in a sword fight against the one remaining Dutchman.

The young Dutchman is holding his own, fighting back with his cutlass and a long knife. He is cornered, with his back against a wall. Jack's men cheer as they watch the three swing their swords against each other for nearly ten minutes. As they near the point of exhaustion, the pace of the fight slows. The Dutchman taunts, "Is that all you have for me, you thieving buggers?" The men watching the duel begin laughing and shouting playful insults at their exhausted comrades. Jack admires the young Dutchman's swordsmanship and fighting spirit. He steps in and says, "Hold your swords, lads." One of his exhausted men yells, "Bloody hell, this one has no quit!"

Jack looks at the young Dutchman and says, "Lad, you've

proved to be a worthy opponent. It would be a shame to end this battle with you run through. Rather than being skewered or meeting the same fate as your crew, I would rather see you live to fight another day alongside my men. What say you— fight alongside us or die alongside them?"

The young Dutchman faces Jack, dripping with sweat. He wipes his brow. "Given the options, captain, I recon I shall join your crew."

"Excellent. Lad, I thought you to be Dutch, but with your use of the Queen's language, it's obvious you are English. What might your name be?"

"Aye, captain, English I am, and my name's Mark Read."

During the night, Jack's crew searches the Dutch ship, taking anything valuable—food, water, gold, extra sails, and liquor. The Dutch ship is too badly damaged to consider salvaging as a prize. After sinking her, the crew expects Jack to continue the deposed Captain Vane's tradition of torturing the captives. Jack tells his crew, "For having the audacity to run from us and to ambush us with a fake surrender, we will avenge our mates who died during battle, with the life of this captain. He shall die by keelhauling. The remaining prisoners were only following their captain's orders and will be given the option of going on the account and joining us or be marooned."

The next morning the Dutch captain and his five men are brought to the ship's deck. The entire crew watches as Jack asks the Dutch captain, "Captain, do you care to make your peace with the Lord before meeting him?" The captain says nothing and simply stares off in the distance.

Jack replies to his silence, "Very well. Lad, be so kind as to lead the brave captain to his fate."

The captain is tied to a rope looped beneath the vessel. He is then thrown overboard on one side of the ship and dragged slowly under the ship's keel to the other side. As the hull is covered in barnacles, the captain is sure to suffer cuts and other injuries before drowning. Six of the Dutch crew joins Jack as shipmates, and the others are marooned on a small island near the northern coast of Carolina.

CHAPTER TWENTY-THREE

THE HOMECOMING

Jack and his crew have been at sea for nearly six months. During this time, they have sailed from the coasts of Jamaica to as far north as Newfoundland. Cruising this route, they have taken three merchant ships and four fishing vessels. Most of their stolen treasures are spent on women and drink when they drop anchor and put in for shore leave in the American colonies. Spending most of their time raiding ships off the coast has drawn the colonial authorities' attention to Jack's name and *The Vanity*. He tells his crew that it might be wise for them to leave American waters in order to put some time and distance between themselves and the growing notoriety they have accrued as a result of recent successes.

They set a course back to the Caribbean. A week later, they arrive in New Providence. As the ship is secured, Jack goes ashore and heads directly to drink at the Goat's Head

Tavern. It is late afternoon and Bay Street is crowded with people. As Jack walks toward the tavern, he takes in the sounds of men singing, mixed laughter, and the faint squeals of prostitutes emanating from bedrooms in the inns that line Bay Street.

Jack thinks to himself how he would rather be in New Providence than anywhere else in the world. On the surface, it appears to be exactly as Jack left it six months earlier, but he knows that things have surely changed with the arrival of the British and their newly planted Governor Rogers.

Since Jack and his crew began their journey back to New Providence, two things have been weighing on his mind. When he walks into the Goat's Head Tavern, he does not know what to expect. It's been over six months since he and his crew marooned Charles Vane. Will Vane have found a way to survive and made his way back to New Providence, waiting for Jack to step into the tavern to exact his revenge? Or will Woodes Rogers' men be waiting for their return, to arrest and hang them for continuing as pirates? Jack faces the tavern door and swings it open with authority. As he steps in, sharp pipe smoke wafts into his nose. He hears loud conversations and laughter. The contrast of walking into the dimly lit tavern from the bright Caribbean sun temporarily blinds Jack, and he strains his eyes to see.

He hears a gruff voice say, "I'll be damned. Look who just walked through the door." A quick surge of panic speeds through Jack's gut as he thinks he may have just been recognized by one of Vane's or Rogers' men. He hears the man say, "Calico Jack, come have a drink with us." His eyes fully adjusted, Jack now sees that the voice he hears comes from a man named Rodney Harwood. Harwood is one of the pirates who have chosen to stay in New Providence and take Governor Rogers up on his offer of a full pardon. The half-drunk men quickly surround Jack, shaking his hand, patting him on the back and offering him drinks. Vane is not among them, nor is any of Rogers' men. There is time for Jack to relax and settle in for drinking and telling his stories about his adventures on the high seas.

The name Calico Jack Rackham and *The Vanity* have become the talk of New Providence. Word spread about their show of defiance by refusing the governor's pardon and the gutsy move that Jack made, passing so close to his ships on his way out to sea. He joins the group of men at a table off to the side of the bar.

He spins his tales and he sees the sunlight illuminate the bar as another patron enters the front door. The light causes Jack to turn his head as he continues telling his stories. He sees a scrawny man enter and walk toward the bar. Just as Jack begins to turn his full attention back to his audience, he catches a glimpse of the flowing motion of a woman's dress trailing the gentleman who has just entered. In a moment that seems to be suspended in time, Jack and the woman lock eyes as she passes the spot where Jack and the others are seated. Jack continues telling his story but cannot pull his eyes away from the woman. He instinctively knows that there is something different about her. She is incredibly beautiful and mysterious. He senses a hint of danger. The couple who have just entered the bar is none other than James and Anne Bonny, venturing into the tavern for an early evening drink. Jack watches the couple as they take their drinks from the bar to a small table on the other side of the large room. As they take their seats, James's back is toward Jack, while Anne faces him.

Jack continues his story. He interjects more expression and raises his voice just enough to make his presence known. The increased volume of his voice has no effect. The fine lady seated across the room does not look his way. He continues, but this time even louder and with more exuberance. Looking annoyed, James rolls his eyes and says to Anne, "That warthog is a loud mouthed imbecile," and takes another large gulp of his ale. Anne then looks in the direction of the booming voice, noticing that he seems to be looking directly at her.

He continues to talk and stare in her direction. She thinks that he must be focusing on something behind her. She looks over her shoulder to see what this man might be looking at. She turns back and he winks at her. At this moment, Anne realizes that he is focused on her. A few minutes pass as Jack finishes his story. Anne sees him become more animated and hears him say, "I then stood nose-to-nose and looked into his eyes and said, 'Captain, if you do not choose to oblige me by divulging where your ship's valuables are hidden, then I shall feed your Portuguese arse to the sharks!'" A few more discernible words are spoken and after a few seconds of silence, laughter explodes from all the men at the table.

The man pushes his chair back from the table and walks toward the bar. As he gets closer to Anne and James, she sees that he is wearing brightly colored clothes, a long red coat with large, polished brass buttons, and a black tricorn hat sprouting a large red feather from one side. Before reaching the bar, the man places his order for three rums and tosses a coin on the bar top. Anne thinks to herself, *This man is full of himself, and rightly so. He's handsome and has a commanding presence.* Jack walks from the bar toward Anne and James's table, holding two glasses of rum in one hand and the third in his other hand. James notices that Anne is tracking something with her eyes. He turns and is startled to see a red coat only a foot from his face. He looks at the man and sees that he holds drinks in his hands. Jack says, "Sorry mate, my apologies for startling you so. I noticed the two of you sitting at this table, and thought I would take the liberty to introduce myself." Jack does not take his eyes off Anne. She notices this and stares back into Jack's eyes.

James notices their eyes locked onto each other and responds, "I'm James Bonny, and this is my wife." The tone in James's voice causes Jack to redirect his attention to James.

"Well, Mister and Mrs. Bonny, I am pleased to make your acquaintance. I thought that since we have never met, I would offer the two of you a drink. My name is Jack Rackham, but I'm better known as Calico Jack Rackham. I captain the ship known as *The Vanity* that sails from this port." As Jack introduces himself, he presents a gentleman's bow. This is not one of the half-done bows that Anne has seen so many men do time and again, but a real gentleman's bow that includes Jack removing his hat and crossing it in front of his body. She has seen this more traditional and elaborate bow only a few times in her life, as it is most commonly made by noblemen and British royalty. In response, Anne smiles. Her instincts tell her that in this place and time there are no true gentlemen, no matter how Calico Jack Rackham presents himself. She knows that he is a wolf in sheep's clothing, and it is obvious that this wolf has his eyes on her. At this moment, she knows that he wants her and that she wants him.

Chapter Twenty-Four

Taking Anne

James begins to drift back to his unfaithful ways. He has tried to be true to Anne, but lacks the moral fortitude to do so. He also has made several attempts to stop working for Governor Rogers as one of his many informants. James thinks that if he does not return with information, the governor will forget about him and their agreement over time. This is not the case. When James does not report weekly with information, Rogers' men visit him. They inform him that if he does not continue the flow of information, he will soon find himself with no more worries, meaning that he will soon be dead. Jack begins noticing that Anne is coming to the Goat's Head Tavern more and more without her husband. Each night that Anne is alone Jack finds his way to her table. After having only a few conversations, Jack and Anne begin to realize that they are more than simply attracted to each other. The strong connection between them is obvious and something they can't explain. The two don't discuss their feelings; instead, they hold their thoughts. Anne thinks to herself, *If an affair with Jack is inevitable, fate will bring us together.*

As they sit together night after night, their conversations continue to grow, each one lasting longer than the last. Jack cannot figure out how he can be so consumed with Anne while, uncharacteristically, not trying to take her to bed. For the first time in his life, Jack has completely fallen for a woman. His instincts tell him that this woman is different, his equal, and he knows he has never met another woman like her.

He thinks to himself, *What a paradox this woman is—a Pandora's box filled with beauty and intelligence while having a scoundrel's tongue and a healthy appetite for rum.* Jack also senses an undercurrent of recklessness in Anne. This contrasting combination both confuses and intrigues him.

Anne confides in Jack, telling him two things, one that he already knows and the second that he suspects. "I am not happy being the wife of James Bonny. I know that James is still working as an informant for the governor. After he was given his pay last week, we drank at the tavern, and later that evening as he slept, I counted his money. There was too much for an honest laborer. He's been telling me that he works with others to restore the governor's headquarters, and since he sometimes works late into the night, he says that he finds it easier to sleep there so he can awake early the next morn. When he returns after being gone, I ask him about the work that keeps him away from me. He stumbles over his words and gets violently angry. James may think he is fooling me with his lies, but he is not. He's a god-awful liar. I cannot stand even to look at him. I know that when he's not sleeping by my side, he's bedding somewhere else with a whore. I also know that as an informant, he gives the governor information that betrays the people we know, including those we call our friends. James sickens me."

After hearing Anne express how she despises James, Jack sees a window of opportunity and says, "Annie."

Before Jack can utter another word, he is interrupted by a light chuckle from Anne. She says, "Sorry, Jack, but the only other person that has ever called me Annie is my father."

Jack smiles, pauses and continues, "Annie, after listening to you telling me about your feelings for your imbecile husband, you should take stock of the fact that he will not change and that your marriage to him will never bring you happiness."

Anne looks into Jack's eyes and says, "Captain, it sounds like you know what will bring me happiness."

"Aye, lass, I would wager the king's crown jewels that I do." Anne knows exactly what Jack will tell her if she asks what he thinks will make her happy. She simply smiles and does not reply. At this moment, Jack makes the decision that Anne should be by his side and not that of James Bonny. He begins planning a captain's strategy. He plots scenarios that will permanently separate the two. He quickly concludes that the best way to accomplish this goal is to remove James permanently from Anne's life. James must die. Jack will have one of his crew ambush James, cut his throat, tie a weight to him, and dump his corpse into the sea.

No one would think twice about the reasons why James disappeared. Jack knows that the British will assume that one of the men James betrayed has taken revenge and killed him, or that he fled New Providence to escape being under the governor's control. Everyone will assume that someone did James in. He is also confident that she will not care if James suddenly were to disappear. Having him anchored to the bottom of the bay as fish food would thwart any chance of the two changing their minds about each other and possibly reconciling in the future.

The first step in Jack's plan is to order two of his crew to follow both James and Anne. Jack wants daily reports on the routes that James takes and where he eats, drinks, and sleeps. This information will provide Jack with the most opportune time and place to set step two in motion. Jack has Anne followed simply to protect her from harm. In his mind, he is confident that she can hold her own against most men, but he also knows that her beauty and curves are plenty to tempt many a rogue.

The man keeping an eye on James informs him that James has a predictable schedule and always travels the same routes. He also confirms Anne's suspicions. Jack already knows that James is an informant for the governor's office. The only reason why James has not been killed for his betrayals is that he's worth more to the pirates living than dead. The remaining pirate crews still operating from New Providence use James to their advantage, conversing with James to feed him misinformation that he delivers to Rogers. Jack also learns that James is a creature of habit. When James does not return home to Anne, he spends the night with one of three prostitutes. Jack's man informs him that James is now heading to the Goat's Head Tavern. Jack knows that Anne also will be there and plans to be there as well. He enters the tavern to find that he has arrived before Anne or James. He settles in with a bottle of rum at the table where he and Anne usually sit. A half hour passes before James enters. He has a determined look on his face as he approaches the bar and orders a drink. James slams the drink and orders another. He looks around the tavern and notices Jack seated at the table in the corner, where the light is low.

The barkeep continues to pour James drinks. After his fifth drink in less than five minutes, the barkeep comments, "Bonny, you seem to be in quite a hurry today." In response to his comment, James flashes the bartender a sarcastic smile, puts his glass on the bar top, and demands, "Gimme another!" James looks around the tavern again and notices that Jack has not taken his eyes off him since he walked into the establishment. Jack has thoughts of killing James on the spot, but does not act. Jack's focus on James is abruptly interrupted by bright sunlight flooding the bar as the tavern doors open. Anne walks in with her head turned toward the corner to see if Jack is sitting at their table. She looks at Jack and smiles, only to notice that something is wrong. Jack does not acknowledge her, and she sees that he is staring straight ahead at the bar. Anne turns to see James staring at her with an angry expression on his face. He walks up to her, grabs her by her arm, and says, "You're coming with me." James leads Anne outside the bar and pulls her across Bay Street into their room at the inn. He slings her body across the room and onto their bed and slams the door. Anne immediately stands up from the bed and says, "James, it would be in your best interest not to touch me again." She then asks, "What has happened?"

"While working in the guv-nuh's headquarters this morning, two guards led me into his office for questioning. I was asked to take a seat, and the guv-nuh told me, 'Mister Bonny, it was brought to my attention that you are married to a woman who I have been asked to arrest for assaulting a woman named Elizabeth Lawes. She is the sister-in-law of Nicholas Lawes, the governor of Jamaica.' I responded with, 'All due respect, Guv-nuh, I know nothing of what you're referring to.'" James tells Anne, "The guv-nuh went on to ask me, 'Are you not the husband of one Anne Bonny?' I told the guv-nuh aye, and he said that you were witnessed striking this woman and knocking two teeth from her head while attending a ball hosted at Chidley Bayard's estate. I laughed and told him that obviously a mistake had been made and that you would never have found yourself in a position to attend a ball hosted by Chidley Bayard. He played me the fool and went on to tell me how you indeed found your way to the ball. He also told me that it's common knowledge that you lived at the Bayard estate and that for nearly two weeks you were bedding with him, as his mistress, until this incident took place, and Bayard had you removed from his home."

Anne puts her hands defiantly on her hips, "So it's wrong for me to sleep with an aristocrat and fine for you to continue to sleep with whores?"

James begins to move deliberately toward Anne as he yells in an enraged voice, "Woman, you will not make me look like a fool again."

Anne can sense what is about to happen, quickly grabs a heavy pewter candlestick holder from the table next to her and raises it, in a ready position to strike James's head. An enormous explosion erupts as the door to their room shatters into splintering pieces of wood. Both James and Anne swing their heads simultaneously toward the unexpected noise. Jack storms into the room and looks at the two frozen figures standing in front of him. James, in a confused state, says, "Rackham?"

Jack turns to Anne and says, "Annie, you are coming with me."

James looks at Anne with disgust. "Ahhh ... bloody hell, Rackham, too? What do you mean by smashing our door to pieces and telling my wife that she is coming with you? Rackham, you have balls the size of a bull. If you turn and leave now, I will not kill you."

Jack looks at Anne and confuses her with an awkward smile. He turns away from her and begins walking toward the doorway. Anne cannot believe what she is seeing; Jack is leaving. James, thinking that Jack heeded his warning and is leaving, looks at Anne and lets out a short, nervous laugh. Anne yells out, "Jack, what are you doing?" Jack stops just short of the doorway, turns, draws his pistol and fires a round into James's thigh. James lets out a sharp yell and grabs his leg as he instantly falls to the floor. The unexpected blast stuns Anne. She watches motionless as Jack slowly walks through a thick cloud of gunpowder smoke and over to James. He replaces his pistol, crouches down and leans toward James to whisper in his ear, "Lad, I have some words for you to reflect upon later after your wife leaves you for me and the surgeon digs the lead ball from your leg. You should never try to call a stronger opponent's hand when it's obvious that he can clearly see a weaker one bluffing before him. To think that just the other day I considered offering you a healthy sum of gold to free Anne from her bad state."

"Rackham, you are the village fool to think that I would consider selling my wife to you."

"Lad, buying your wife from you was a much kinder approach than my first thoughts of killing you and serving your remains to the fish."

"You act as if I should pay you a debt of gratitude for insulting me and shooting my leg. You are insane. You should know that I gave your name and the names of your crew to Guv-nuh Rogers' office. He knows you captain *The Vanity* and its pirate crew. You and your men will surely see your end by hanging. As for you, Anne, Rogers is also sending men to collect you for assaulting the guv-nuh's sister."

Anne interrupts James and corrects him, "James, I assaulted the guv-nuh's sister-in-law, not his sister."

In a fit of frustration James shouts, "Fine! Sister-in-law! The guv-nuh felt badly for the public humiliation you caused me and granted me a favor. Before being thrown in a cell, you will be publicly flogged for your adultery. I suspect that your back will be bloodied and scarred as a constant reminder of your Jezebel ways with Bayard." Jack walks over to James and steps on his hand, twisting his ankle back and forth, grinding it into the wooden floor. With his leg bleeding and his hand being crushed, James releases another painful groan. Jack says in a deep gruff voice, "Mind your tongue, little toad."

Anne sees Jack's hand move to his side and onto the handle of his dagger. He grabs a fistful of James's hair, and in a sharp deliberate motion jerks his head backward, exposing his neck. Jack begins slowly to draw his dagger from its sheath, Anne yells, "No, Jack, let us just leave!" Anne has no misgivings about leaving James on the floor groaning in a pool of his own blood, but she does not want to see Jack murder him by cutting his throat in front of her. She leaves, with Jack, to the sound of James groaning and yelling, "You bloody bastard ... you whore."

As Jack and Anne walk toward the docks, he says, "Annie, if you did not stop me at that very moment you would now be a widow. I cannot lie to you when I say that I would have thoroughly enjoyed ending that informant's life. I am comforted knowing that he is now only a bad memory of your past. I will set sail after darkness falls and leave New Providence behind before the governor's men come for my ship and crew." Jack pauses a brief moment before continuing, "You heard James say that they will also come for you. Knowing this, I cannot leave you behind. I would end my life before allowing them to scar your back. You must leave with me aboard *The Vanity*."

Anne grins, lets out a schoolgirl squeal and launches herself onto Jack, wrapping both her arms and legs around his body. Anne's unexpected action takes Jack completely by surprise. He stumbles to one side, quickly regains his balance and lets out a laugh, "Easy Lass, I reckon your response means you will be sailing with me this eve."

CHAPTER TWENTY-FIVE

THE REVELATION

After leaving New Providence, Jack sets a course to sail northwest up the American coastline. He gives Anne a tour of his ship and shows her all that is below deck. Jack boasts about the ship's eighteen-pound guns and says that he does not know of another ship their size that supports such large guns. She is shown the crew's quarters, where the cook prepares the food and where the valuables they've stolen from other ships are stowed.

They make their way to the upper deck; Jack explains how the ship operates and gives Anne a job description of all the ship's crewmembers. The last stop on his guided tour is the captain's quarters. Jack shows Anne some of the rare valuables that he has claimed from the captains of the ships they've raided. He presents her with a small wooden chest. "Annie, these trinkets are for you." He opens the box to reveal several ornate necklaces, broaches, and rings made of gold and silver. The valuables are encrusted with diamonds and other precious gems.

Anne is at a loss for words and simply says, "Jack, they are beautiful."

He chooses an emerald choker, set in gold the large stone surrounded by diamonds, and clasps it around her throat. Jack smiles and Anne notices that he's focusing on something behind her. She turns to see what Jack is spying. Jack then says in a soft tone, "To end my tour, I would like to present you with the captain's bed, specially made with a goose feather mattress and the finest imported silk sheets made in the orient." Jack pulls Anne close and kisses her. She follows him willingly into his bed. In a moment, she is wearing only the choker as he gently lays her back onto the silken bed. His eyes never leaving hers as he undresses. She thinks she has never been touched so tenderly as he runs his fingers along her side resting them briefly at her hip. Moving toward her inner thigh, he sighs and closes his eyes. She parts her legs slightly, welcoming his fingers to explore her. Kissing his collarbone and running her own hands over his shoulders and down his back, she gasps as his fingers find the warm place where she is aching to feel him. Teasing her, he pauses to circle her nipples with his tongue as he leaves kisses across her chest and over her belly. He breaths her in as his mouth finds her. She has never experienced such a sensation and spreads her legs wider as her back arches toward him. He flicks his tongue against her and discovers the movement and rhythm that bring her to push herself harder against his mouth. Her breath quickens and her hips begin to move in a rhythm over which she has no control. She is falling and flying at once. When she lands, she pulls him to her. Moaning quietly as he enters her body, he moves slowly at first, then more quickly as his arousal intensifies. It is he who is flying, unable to take his eyes from hers.

As he lowers himself next to her, heart pounding, their damp skin touching along the length of their bodies, he feels her rapid breath against his shoulder. Anne's eyes are filled with a look of peaceful contentment as they close but her mind is far from quiet. She has experienced what it is truly to make and feel love. In her life, there have been sexual encounters, but never a bond, a joining, like this one. She has shown him the part of her that has always been hidden just beneath her skin. She has seen, for the first time, part of another's soul resting just behind Jack's eyes. Anne and Jack are not seen outside his cabin for the next two days.

On the third day at sea, Jack appears on deck and gathers his crew. He tells them of the circumstances that brought Anne aboard *The Vanity*. He knows that the men have been talking and that they might disapprove of having a woman aboard the ship. Up to this point, having women sail aboard pirate vessels has been strictly prohibited. After he talks with them, they tell Jack that they will put the matter to a vote. The crew accepts having Anne going on the account with three conditions. One, her presence aboard the ship will, in no way, affect or sway the decisions he makes as the ship's captain. Two, no special treatment will be extended to Anne because of her gender. She will be treated as an equal member of the crew and assigned duties while at sea and in port. Three, in battle she must take up arms and fight against the ship's enemies. Jack addresses his crew and proposes an addendum to their vote. "If this is what you ask, then so be it. I might add that because she will be considered an equal and will be expected to carry out the duties and fight our enemies, she should also be entitled to her equal share of the prizes we take. What say you?"

The crew responds, "Aye."

Anne's lack of training and fighting experience concerns Jack. He knows that putting Anne in a fight against a trained seaman could mean a quick end for her, and immediately begins training her. First, he shows her how to use firearms. She learns to load, aim, and fire flintlock muskets and pistols. He tells her that when fighting at close quarters, without time to reload, she can use them as clubs to disable a rushing man. He also trains Anne effectively to defend herself without weapons by using only her hands and feet. He tells her, "Annie, understand that a strong and determined man cannot be stopped from killing you by hair pulling, scratching, and biting, as most women would do to defend themselves. A well-placed jab to the throat, a thumb pushed deeply into one's eye, or a hard kick to a man's precious jewels can be effective ways to disable him temporarily. Once he is disabled, you must be swift and merciless to end his life. Not moving fast enough to kill a man while he's down or disoriented might give him the chance for one last act of desperation that could have you breathing your own last breath." He also asks Mark Read to help train Anne with a cutlass and the long knife. Jack has seen Mark in action several times and considers him one of the finest swordsmen he has encountered. Mark begins to train Anne daily. As the two train together, Mark taunts her. He wants to teach her how to control her emotions so that they won't cloud her decisions during future fights. Anne begins to love sword fighting and the adrenaline it pumps into her body. During a short period of time, Anne and Mark spend countless hours training. Jack notices that Anne and Mark are talking more and more. He sees the way that Anne laughs and smiles when she is with him and begins keeping a jealous eye on the two. Even though Jack loves Anne dearly, he knows her history and her tendency to switch lovers without remorse.

Jack's suspicions are not unfounded. In the time Mark and Anne have spent together in her training, a unique bond has formed between the two. While naturally intimate in nature, he is, after all, teaching her to defend her own life and potentially take that of another. The relationship has become more than platonic in Anne's mind. While not comprehending why, she finds something about Mark that has led to an easy and comfortable interaction between them. This easiness, along with his soft voice and grace of movement, has grown into a strong, sensual desire in Anne.

After four weeks at sea, *The Vanity* has not found a ship to engage. Jack notices that his men are becoming restless. One evening, while Jack and his officers meet in his cabin to discuss plotting a new course, Anne walks the deck, taking in the sea air. She secs Mark on the other side of the ship, looking at the ocean and approaches him. "Mark, I realized that I have been remiss. You have given up much of your time training me to handle the sword, and through all this, I have not thanked you for all you've done for me." Mark leans forward and puts his hands on the ship's side railing. "Anne, it has been my pleasure. I was a bit worried that in the heat of a fight you would let your temper affect your judgment and let your emotions get the better of you. I've seen others die because they lost control in the heat of a fight. I'm glad to see that you've been able to overcome what could be a disadvantage and turn it into a strength." Anne draws closer to Mark, pressing her chest firmly against his back and putting her hand on top of his. "Mark, the pleasure has been all mine." Anne's flirting catches Mark off guard, and he slowly pulls his hand away and continues to look seaward. He bids her good evening and walks away. Anne's advances continue to intensify over the next week. Jack notices Anne flirting with Mark, and his jealousy builds. She is becoming relentless. One afternoon, she sees Mark and follows him below deck. She approaches him quietly from behind and corners him. "Mark, it is time for you to stop avoiding me and surrender yourself to the inevitable." Anne begins kissing Mark on the neck as he backs into a wall.

Finally, Mark has had enough and cries, "Anne, stop!" He forcefully pushes her away from him. "I must tell you something."

Anne backs away and asks, "What?"

"Anne, you cannot continue with your advances."

Anne replies, "Why might that be?"

"Because I am like you."

"I know ... it's beautiful."

"No, not in that way. I am really like you ... Anne: I am a woman, too."

As she begins to approach him again, Mark says, "I will prove it to you!" Mark begins to unbutton his shirt, pulls it off his back and then begins to unwrap a long coil of bandages that are wrapped around his chest. Anne watches in disbelief as she begins to see skin and then two female breasts released from the wrappings. "My real name is Mary." Anne is speechless, but finally gets her wits about her and says, "Sweet Mother of Jesus! Ha! I knew something was different about you, but I couldn't figure out what it was!" Mark, now Mary, rewraps her chest and begins buttoning her shirt. The door to the storeroom abruptly swings open.

Jack's eyes widen to the size of saucers as the first thing he sees is Mark Read buttoning his shirt. He notices Anne with a guilty look on her face, as if she has been caught in the act.

He is enraged and losing control. "Aha! Just as I suspected! I've seen the way you two have been looking at and talking to each other. Annie, your bad habits are beginning to reveal themselves over time. As for you, Mark Read..." Jack draws his sword and wields a fierce swing as

Mary takes a quick step backward to avoid his blade. Anne yells, "Jack, it's not what you think!" Mary draws her sword and is in a ready position. "Captain Rackham, if you intend to kill me, then you must know that I intend to give you one hell of a fight before one of us falls." Jack lunges, thrusting his sword forward toward Mary's chest as their two swords connect with a loud clang. Anne yells again, "Jack, stop fighting her!" Jack, about to swing again, realizes that Anne has just said, "Stop fighting *her*."

Anne continues, "Jack, Mark's not a man, he's a she!" Jack pauses for a split second and looks bewildered. "What, you mean he's a woman? I don't believe you."

Anne looks at Mary, "Mary, you need to show him."

"I would rather die from his blade."

"Mary, just show him!"

In disgust, Mary throws her sword down hard on the wooden floor, yells "Bloody hell" and begins to unbutton her shirt. She unravels the bandages around her chest to reveal her breasts once again. A surprised Jack puts his sword back into its sheath. "I'll be damned, another hellcat aboard my ship!" All tension leaves the room. Jack lets out a brief laugh and shakes his head in confusion. "Why the charade, my dear?"

"Captain, it's a long twisted tale that I'm sure won't interest you."

"Lass, let me be the judge of what I find interesting. Tell me your tale."

CHAPTER TWENTY-SIX

THE CHARADE

Mary tells Jack and Anne, "My mother's husband was a seaman. Before I was born, he left my mother and infant half-brother to board a merchant ship bound for America. The ship never made it to its destination. It was presumed that the ship sank *en route* somewhere in the Atlantic, and all aboard were lost. A year of mourning left my mother tired and lonely. She met a man, and they had a relationship. Soon after that, she found herself pregnant with me. The man who fathered me abandoned her after learning that she was pregnant. Shortly after I was born, my older brother died of a fever at the age of three. With my father gone, and with the death of my brother, my mother feared that her mother-in-law would cut off the monthly financial support she had been sending us. My mother told me that if my grandmother learned that her family's bloodline was lost with the death of my brother, she would no longer feel responsible for continuing to support us. Without having enough income for us to survive, my mother had an idea to disguise me as a boy to trick our neighbors and my grandmother into thinking that her deceased grandson was still alive to carry on the family name. My grandmother's advancing age kept her from traveling from her home in London to where we lived in Devonshire. Knowing this, my mother figured that enough time would pass for me to grow and assume the identity of my deceased brother. My mother did what she had to do in order for us to survive. She told me what she was making me do and why. I really have seldom shown any feminine qualities. I never owned a dress, and I was forbidden to speak in public. My mother provided me with a fine education from our home. I assume that she did not want me attending school with others my age, in fear that I might slip and give up our little secret.

When I was three years old, we traveled to London to visit my grandmother. I was later told that the ruse was successful and my grandmother did not question a thing. My name was Mark Read, and I knew nothing different. After twelve years, my grandmother died, and the family's money ran dry. By this time, I had accepted playing the role of a male, and it became second nature to me.

"With few options, I continued with what I knew best. I began working as a footboy for a nobleman on the naval docks in Plymouth. I found that continuing my disguise afforded me countless more options to gain employment. Eventually, I found a better-paying opportunity in Flanders as a soldier in a cavalry regiment. Through training, I learned as much as I could to handle all types of weaponry. I became a skilled marksman with both the musket and pistol, but my passion was wielding a blade. To me, the sword seemed to be an elegant weapon, one that required a greater level of skill to master. During my service, I met and fell in love with a fellow soldier. It was something that I did not expect to happen, but it did. It was very difficult wanting to share my feelings for a man when he thought me also to be a man. I thought that he could never care for me, if he knew how I had deceived him. I eventually built up enough nerve to reveal myself to him, just as I just did with you. At first, he was confused and angry. I told him about my past and how I grew up playing the role of a male. He kept my secret, and eventually he realized that he had feelings for me, too. We were not sure how our commanding officer would take the news of my ruse. We considered deserting, but knew that the crime was punishable by death. Our best option was to tell our commanding officer my story and ask for his understanding. We requested a private meeting with him in his quarters. He granted us permission to speak freely. I began telling him all about my past. He listened attentively, and being a man of reason, he accepted my story as the truth and showed leniency toward our predicament. We were unable to stay in active service as newlyweds, so he granted us both an honorable discharge so that we could embark on a new life together. Before we left and were married, the regiment was informed of this most unusual alliance. The commanding officer encouraged each soldier in the regiment to give us a small token of his appreciation as a parting gift for serving the regiment. The collection was generous. After leaving the regiment in 1697, we purchased an inn frequented by travelers and soldiers. The inn was called The Three Horseshoes. We enjoyed a happy life together as husband and wife. One evening, while serving the inn's patrons, I found myself receiving unwanted advances from a soldier. In defense of my honor, my husband challenged the soldier to a duel."

"As quickly as our life together began, it ended. My husband died the very next day of a gunshot wound to his stomach he received during the duel. My love was gone, and the war was ending, and the inn's regular customers, being soldiers, returned to their homes. Business slowed and eventually the inn failed. Once again, I found myself without money. With no ties to hold me, I burned the inn to the ground and went back to what I knew best. As Mark Read, I once again called upon my skills of disguise. I joined a Dutch merchant ship, as a deckhand, bound for the West Indies. As our ship sailed, you, captain, and your fine crew raided and overtook our vessel, and here I am today."

Jack and Anne stand silently for a minute, still processing the incredible tale that they have just heard.

Jack breaks the silence by saying, "Lass, your survival skills impress me. As I see it, we have two choices to consider. It was an unorthodox move for me to bring Anne aboard my ship the way I did. My decision to do so could have cost me my command if the crew did not vote in favor of her sailing with us. I cannot knowingly allow you to remain disguised as a male shipmate, although you play the role well. I had no clue, and I am sure that the crew has no clue, either. As the ship's captain, I will have to tell them what I know now and ask them to decide. They will vote to keep you as a member of the crew or put you ashore when we anchor at the next colony. I will try to sway their vote, considering that you are the best swordsman aboard the ship."

Jack gathers the crew and tells them what he has learned. The crew is dumbfounded to learn that Mark Read is really a woman.

One crewmember shouts, "You mean he is a she? Are you positive?"

Another shouts, "What be her name?"

Another, "You mean she's a sheep in wolf's clothing?"

The sound of laughter is heard among the men. Another crewmember says, "I have not seen many men who can fight as ferociously and with the skill that she has with a sword."

The crew votes to keep Mary aboard *The Vanity* as an equal.

Chapter Twenty-Seven

No Wind

As *The Vanity* sails toward the northern coast of America, the wind has stopped blowing, everything becoming deathly still. It has been three days and nights without even a slight breeze to move the ship's sails. With no wind, the ship's motion remains almost completely frozen. The ocean's current causes its only movement, and the stillness of the air in the searing heat from the persistent summer sun is stifling. The crew's bodies lose water faster than it can be replenished. All on deck do their best to find what little shade is available. Jack steps out of his cabin, wiping the beading sweat from his forehead. "Bloody mess this is. No wind and hotter than a brick oven!" He turns to his quartermaster and says quietly, "Dear God, Mister Corner, we've sailed straight into Hell."

"Aye captain, it's beginning to feel like what I imagine Hell to be."

"When was the last inventory taken of our remaining

fresh water?"

"Captain, an inventory was taken early this morning. The levels have dropped significantly, much lower than they should be considering your order to begin rationing two days ago."

"Then the men have been taking more water than they have been rationed. I know how to deter them." Jack walks across the deck where Ajani, Anne, and Mary are sitting in the shade that the mast is casting. As he approaches them, they stop talking and turn their heads to listen to what he has to say.

"Ahhh, I see you're enjoying today's balmy weather. It seems that some of the men have decided to take more water than what has been allotted to them. They need to be stopped. I want you three to stand guard over the rations below deck. Use barrels to block the corridor's access to the hold where the remaining fresh water is stored. Post yourselves behind the barrels with your weapons in plain view. The only crew allowed to pass will be our cook and myself. If any man approaches you, relay my orders that access to the hold is forbidden. If they persist, you are to draw your weapons and issue a stern warning to retreat. If they disobey, you are to fire upon them. Shoot low to wound, I don't want a shipmate to die because he's insane with thirst."

Mary and Anne reply, "Aye captain." Jack looks to Ajani, who nods his head to indicate his understanding of Jack's orders. Jack walks back to the quartermaster and tells him,

"Mister Corner, continue strict rations on all liquids, including rum, and cut food rations to half of what they are now. With the lack of water and the men sweating as much as they are, eating food will only cause their bodies to dry faster."

"Aye captain."

"I suffered through a very similar experience a number of years ago when I was a deckhand aboard a merchant ship sailing from England to America. I recall that no wind, heat, and idle men caused tensions to run high. Some men went crazy with thirst and snapped in only a few days. Even the most docile men become uncharacteristically aggressive when thirsty. When tensions run high, weaker-minded men can reach their breaking point quickly."

The crew of *The Vanity* sees Jack as all that a captain should be. He seems unaffected by the searing heat—calmly in control and mentally tougher than everyone else. In reality, his insecurities of serving as the ship's commander begin to wear on his mind. He knows all too well that on a pirate ship, when times are good, all is good, and when times are bad, bad things happen. Even though he cannot control nature, the crew he commands can turn on him in a flash, placing blame on him and his officers for charting a course that has put them into their present predicament. Jack knows that if he does not do something quickly to divert his men's attention, he may find himself, along with those who remain loyal to him, cast adrift in a longboat, marooned to suffer certain death.

Anne, Mary, and Ajani go below deck and begin moving barrels to set up a barrier. They block the corridor leading to the room where the remaining fresh water, rum, and dried goods are stored. They place six barrels side-by-side and take their position behind the barricade. All is quiet during the day and into the night. To pass the time, Anne and Mary try to teach Ajani how to speak English as he teaches them his African language of Bantu. The women draw animals and objects on the ship's wood floor with pieces of charcoal. Since Ajani was raised as a part of a primitive African tribe, he is still unfamiliar with many of the objects the two draw for him. He recognizes many of the animals and calls them out by their name in his native tongue.

Mary draws a bird and points to it and says, "Ajani, bird." Ajani looks at the drawing, cocks his head, looks at Anne and Mary, smiles and says, "Pojo!" Anne and Mary try to hold back their laughter. Mary repeats and says, "Ajani, bird!" Ajani contorts his lips awkwardly and says, "Ba ... bi ... bea ... birrrd." Anne says in an excited voice, "Good Ajani!" Hours pass and the three grow tired. They decide to take turns sleeping. While two stay awake and guard the water, the other sleeps for one hour. Ajani and Anne take the first shift. While Mary sleeps, Ajani softly sings tribal songs. In the background, they hear the voices of shipmates bedding down for the night. They hear sharp cracks and moans caused by the constant weight of the ocean pushing against the wooden planks of the ship's hull.

Mary rustles and awakes from her catnap. "What did I

miss? No water poachers?"

"Mary, shhhh, it's been deathly quiet until a moment ago."

Anne nods her head to direct Mary's attention to Ajani. Mary looks to see Ajani standing perfectly still, seemingly ready for any man who might present himself. Beads of sweat drip from his forehead but are diverted from flowing into his eyes by his protruding brows.

The trio waits silently for the sound of anyone approaching them. They hear a sudden shuffle. They turn their heads simultaneously, as though the movement were choreographed. Ajani slowly raises and hurdles his spear. Anne lets out a gasp as the spear flies twenty feet over the top of a row of barrels and with a sharp thud lodges into the wooden hull. Ajani turns to Anne and Mary and in an excited voice exclaims, "Dead!" They don't know what to expect as he runs to his spear, grabs the shaft and gives it a short but deliberate tug to release its embedded blade from the hull. The spear gives a little kick as it is freed. Ajani turns to the women and presents a dead rat dangling from the spear's blade. They all begin laughing. Mary says, "Bloody hell, when you launched your spear I thought that you had surely killed one of our mates. I am sure that once the captain issued his orders for us to stand guard, the crew spread the word. They know that they would have no chance to gain access to the water. No matter how thirsty a man is they would not want to risk a fight with us."

The next morning the sun rises early, and Jack asks his quartermaster and navigator to join him in his quarters. He offers the officers a seat as he takes a set of large oceanic maps from a wooden chest and places them on the table. The men gather round. "Richard, George, I've been thinking about the precarious position that we are in. With no currents or wind to move our ship, there is no telling how long we will sit baking in the sun. Our fresh water supplies are low and the men are becoming agitated, so much so that if a rat shits next to them they might snap. We need to keep them busy and make an effort to better our situation." Jack unrolls a set of high sea Atlantic maps, points to a spot on the map and asks his navigator George Featherston, "George, do you agree that this is where our ship sits?"

"Aye captain, based upon my knowledge of the course we set and my study of night sky, I believe so."

"Good, then we should be no more than sixty miles from the Gulf Stream's current. Since Vane added our additional guns, the side ports are useless for dropping oars. We will have to lower our longboats and have our mates pull us into swifter waters. The water we sit in now is too deep and the current too slow. We might as well be anchored. Richard, what be your position on this?"

"Captain, having the men pull the ship sixty miles in still water will be a task. With our fresh water supplies nearly depleted, we could lose men, but sitting here waiting for better fortune to find us also poses a risk."

"And you George?"

"Captain, our calculations could also lack accuracy. It could be that we are further off course than we imagine. We know that the Gulf Stream is due west. However, we could very well be a hundred miles away from these swifter moving waters."

"As captain of this ship, I do not want to risk losing crew members, but the risk of sacrificing a few, for the good of all, makes me weigh on the side of pulling us to better water. Then, we will put into the nearest port to water our men. Mister Corner, do you agree?"

"Aye captain."

"And Mister Featherston, What say you?"

"Aye captain."

"Then it is settled; I will address the crew and place their options to a vote."

Minutes later, the order is issued for all hands on deck. Jack stands before his crew and begins speaking. "Mates, Mother Nature has put us under her cruel thumb. Our situation can become dire if the current conditions remain unchanged. We are faced with two options. First, we can bide our time, and hope that winds will eventually find our sails. If we decide to stay put and the sun continues its assault on us, and the wind does not find us for several more days, we could be doomed. Or, we can lower our longboats and pull *The Vanity* to swifter currents that we estimate less than sixty miles from our present position. Pulling *The Vanity* miles to the Gulf currents will be a difficult, backbreaking task. But on our way to more forgiving waters, we might be so lucky as to find some wind. Our fresh water supply is nearly gone. The only solace I can offer you is our remaining reserve of rum. If you decide to row our way out of this mess, taking in the rum will ease the pain that your body will endure on our way to the swifter currents."

Jack hears the grumbling voices of his men as they talk to each other. The tone of their voices is low and angry. Jack also knows that his crew could include a third option, to relieve him of his command and set him adrift. Before addressing his crew, Jack decided to divert the crew's attention away from him. Even though his thoughts seemed comical in his mind, he decided to place blame on cruel Mother Nature. After all, she's really the one who controls the elements. Jack figured that this approach might cause his men to think about her instead of him when casting their votes. He has offered his crew all of the remaining rum aboard the ship, in order to sweeten the deal. After only ten minutes, the crew finishes casting their votes. The quartermaster tallies their votes and announces that they will be lowering the longboats and pulling *The Vanity* in an attempt to find more forgiving waters. With the decision to row, Jack orders his men to take shifts pulling the ship using the longboats and oars. He tells them that all crewmembers will participate in this task, including the captain, his officers, and the women aboard. As the first shift of men prepares to leave the ship, Jack tells them, "Lads, if the wind cannot find *The Vanity*, then we will find the wind for her." Four longboats are lowered into the still water. Eight men pile into each boat with five bottles of rum. They tie various lengths of towing ropes to the bow of the 65-foot and 113-ton ship. After positioning the boats ahead of the ship, Jack gives the signal to begin rowing. After the first six strokes, the ship reluctantly begins to inch forward. Jack hears the men grunting as they strain to move the large vessel and create forward momentum. Through the grunting, he hears one of the men begin singing the lyrics to a popular sea shanty, "*Drunken Sailor.*" Jack smiles, turns to his quartermaster, and says, "Mister Corner, I believe that we will conquer this situation."

The man belts out loudly,

"What'll we do with a drunken sailor?

What'll we do with a drunken sailor?

What'll we do with a drunken sailor?

Earl-aye in the morning?"

The other mates join in with the chorus:

"Put him in the long boat 'til he's sober ...

Shave his belly with a rusty razor ...

Put him in bed with the captain's daughter ...

That's what we'll do with the drunken sailor!"

The man continues,

"What'll we do with a drunken sailor?

What'll we do with a drunken sailor?

What'll we do with a drunken sailor?

Earl-aye in the morning?"

The other men continue the chorus even louder.

"Beat him with a cat 'til his back is bleedin' ...

Soak 'em in oil 'til he sprouts a flipper ...

Put him in the bilge and make him drink it ...

That's what we'll do with the drunken sailor!"

The singing goes on for hours as the men continue to sing popular sea shanties and row until they are eventually relieved by the next shift of men.

The sun sets and the rowing continues through the night. All aboard are fatigued and reaching the point of exhaustion. When not rowing on the longboats, most men board the ship and within minutes, collapse into comatose sleep. Being that rum is the only remaining liquid left for them to drink, a strong stench of rum envelops the ship's decks.

Jack confers with his navigator. "Mister Featherston, how far do you reckon we have pulled this bloody ship?"

"Captain, I would estimate nearly thirty miles."

"I don't know how much longer the men can continue this pace with only ..." Jack pauses as a distracted look covers his face and then finishes his sentence. "... rum in their bellies."

"Captain, are you ..."

Jack interrupts Featherston, putting his index finger to his lips, while motioning with his other hand for him to stop speaking. "Do you feel that?"

"Feel what, captain?"

"Wind!"

They freeze and look skyward toward the ship's main sail. As they stare at the sail, they see it begin to flap gently as a gust of wind begins to blow. The two begin to laugh uncontrollably. Jack grabs Featherston by his shoulders and as he laughs, yells, "Wind! Featherston, we've found wind!" Jack runs to the front of the ship as a stronger gust of wind blows his hat off his head. He yells to his crew still pulling the ship in their longboats. "Lads, do you feel that? That would be what we set out to find. Stop rowing! We have just conquered that bitch Mother Nature!" *The Vanity* and crew find their way to Norfolk, Virginia, where they put into port and replenish their supplies.

Chapter Twenty-Eight

A Meeting of Captains

On the last week of February 1720, *The Vanity* reached the upper coast of the American colonies. The ship sailed into Boston Harbor, with plans to spend two nights and three days there. In 1720, the population of American colonists reached 500,000. Boston was still the largest city with 12,000 people, followed by Philadelphia with 10,000 and New York with 7,000. Jack loved the atmosphere of larger colonial cities. They reminded him of London, but less formal and less pretentious. He knew that Anne would be turning twenty years old on Tuesday, the eighth day of March. He had plans to surprise her with a birthday gift and tour all three cities, beginning with Boston, then working their way down the colonial coast to New York City and Philadelphia. She told him that growing up in Charles Towne, she often read about the colonies' three largest cities and always wanted to visit them.

It was late evening when the ship dropped anchor. Jack had informed his crew that beginning the next day, they would stay in Boston for two nights to allow the crew to take shore leave in shifts. Half of the crew would go ashore the first night and the other for the second night. Jack would also use the time in Boston to replenish their supplies for his plans to sail back to Caribbean waters.

Just after one o'clock in the morning, Jack and Anne were awakened from a sound sleep by the sound of a knock at their cabin door. Anne wakes up from the persistent noise, grabs Jack's shoulder, and shaking it, whispering, "Wake up. Someone is at our door." Jack rolls over and with his face down and buried in his pillow, growls, "Sweet Jesus, what? What the bloody hell is it?" He lifts himself out of bed and makes his way across the pitch-black cabin. Banging his knee against the corner of a low table and yelling, "Damn!" Jack reaches the door and swings it open. Jack sees his quartermaster standing before him. "Mister Corner, if you would be so kind as to tell me what could possibly be so important that it could not wait until after the sun is risen?"

"Begging your pardon captain, a ship has been spotted approaching our position from the mouth of the Harbor."

"What type of ship?"

"By its profile, it appears to be a British frigate. With no moon tonight, I cannot be certain who steers it, friend or foe. I thought it best to wake and inform you."

"I doubt that, without our flag raised, the British would be headed our way and seriously doubt that Guv-nuh Rogers would be so ambitious to send a frigate to search the Atlantic for us. Enough said: I will join you on the deck."

Jack closes the cabin door and Anne inquires, "What is it?"

"It seems that a royal frigate is sailing toward us. I am sure we are merely in their path as they are entering the harbor and will pass us."

"Then why does your voice sound the way it does before you head into a fight?"

As Jack dresses, he replies, "Annie, go back to sleep, I will be back to join you soon."

Jack joins his quartermaster and a few others on deck to observe the approaching ship. Corner hands Jack a spyglass to get a better look at the ship as it approaches. "They do not fly a flag. If they were British with intentions to engage us, they would be flying the Union Jack. Since we do not have our flag raised, they will not attack us until they understand that we are not a Dutch merchant vessel. We should simply remain anchored in our current position to see what they do."

As Jack and his crew expect the frigate to continue into the harbor, the frigate slows, comes to a complete stop and drops anchor. The rumble of the anchor's large chain can be heard in the stillness of the night. Jack observes, "Dropping anchor near us is unexpected. I think that they have chosen to play a game of cat and mouse with us and observe us during the light of day. Mister Corner, at this point, they seem to pose no threat. I will be in my cabin, wake me if you observe any unusual movements aboard that ship."

At first light, Corner sends a shipmate to wake Jack. Jack makes his way to the deck, and asks, "Mister Corner, what do you see?"

Corner replies, "Captain, the frigate remains anchored in the same position. However, I have observed some activity on their deck and spotted several of their crew observing us, none of whom are wearing British naval uniforms."

"They are not British if they are not wearing uniforms. The Brits would never be caught outside in plain view without being properly attired."

Jack takes the spyglass and suddenly sees that they are raising their flag. "Lads, we will know in a moment who these visitors be. They are raising their flag. Prepare to raise our flag. Have all hands ready for battle stations upon my command and men at the ready to raise our anchor."

Jack laughs as he sees a black flag being raised on the frigate. As he continues to look through the spyglass, he says, "I'll be damned, they be pirates. Mister Corner, have our flag raised so that they know who we are." *The Vanity's* flag, with its skull and crossed sabers, is quickly aloft. Jack looks once more and sees one of its crew give a wave to signify that they have seen *The Vanity's* flag. Jack looks, once again, at the other flag and drops his spyglass. "That's not just any pirate ship. I recognize that flag. It is none other than Bartholomew Roberts' ship. Mister Corner, prepare to drop a boat. I will need you and three others to row to Captain Roberts' ship and extend an invitation for him and his officers to be my guests aboard our ship for dinner this evening." Jack is flabbergasted that he will have the opportunity to meet Bartholomew Roberts in person.

Bartholomew is a living legend. He is considered the most successful and feared pirate captain roaming the seas. It's believed that he has taken over 300 ships. He is the pirate most wanted by all of the major powers.

Jack postpones shore leave for one day. He orders his crew to clean *The Vanity*, making her spotless in preparation for his dinner guests. His cook creates a feast fit for kings, and Jack selects the finest wines and rum from his private reserves.

In their quarters, Anne says nothing as she watches Jack nervously talk to himself while combing through his wardrobe. He begins laying combinations of shirts, coats, pants, and hats onto their bed. He pauses and notices that Anne is staring at him and asks her, "What?"

"Jack you act as if you are a nervous girl meeting a boy for the first time."

"My Dear, you obviously do not comprehend the magnitude of this event. Captain Bartholomew Roberts is the king of piracy. He is truly considered royalty amongst the brethren."

"I see. Will I be invited to this event?"

"Annie, I would have you by my side if I could. However,

it is not customary to have a female dine in these types of situations."

"Nor is it customary to have women aboard a pirate ship, is it Jack?" Anne storms from their cabin as Jack lets out a loud mocking laugh.

At 6:30 that evening, the crew assembles on the deck as Captain Roberts and his contingent of officers board the ship. Jack extends his hand and says, "Captain Roberts, welcome aboard *The Vanity*. I am Captain Jack Rackham. It is a true honor to make your acquaintance."

"It is always good to meet others in the trade. Your name, Calico Jack Rackham, and the name of your vessel have become increasingly well known." Jack smiles with pride as he introduces his officers and leads the group of hardened pirates to dine. They eat, drink and tell stories well into the evening. One story leads to another as the two groups progressively try to outdo each other. Hours into their conversation, Jack realizes that he has run out of experiences to relate. He and his crew have taken a miniscule amount of ships in comparison to Roberts and his crew. From this point forward, Jack simply decides to ask Roberts questions and listen to his responses. "I heard that you knew Edward Teach quite well."

"Ahhh, yes. Teach, or Blackbeard, as he liked to call himself. Teach was a good man, a hard drinker and a bit crazed, but a solid navigator and commander. I was always amazed and found it somewhat humorous that he felt it necessary to go to such great lengths to make himself look fiercer in times of battle. He placed lengths of rope between his head and hat and lit the frayed ends before jumping aboard the ships they attacked. He once told me that he enjoyed doing this so much because of the wide-eyed looks he received from surprised seamen. He told me of a time when sailing off the coast of Jamaica: while he and his crew were drinking heavily, they spotted a Spanish merchant vessel. In their drunken fervor, they attacked the ship. Before jumping aboard the Spanish deck, he decided to include the lengths of frayed rope in his long, black beard in addition to the ropes atop his head. He lit the ends of the ropes, and as he jumped onto the edge of the ship, the unmistakable smell of burning hair hit his nostrils. His beard was ablaze. He quickly jumped back onto his ship and doused his head in a bucket of water." Roberts' tale causes all at the dinner table to roar with laughter. "In the fall of 1718, Teach returned from sea to his favorite hideaway off Ocracoke Island. He hosted a huge, wild gathering with dancing, drinking, and bonfires. Many pirates sailed to the island to attend the three-day event. I joined the gathering with four of my ships, and I believe that I remember seeing Charles Vane."

Jack responds, "Yes, you are correct. We enjoyed two days of drinking, feasting and song. At that time I was Vane's quartermaster."

"I later heard that news of the gathering reached Alexander Spotswood, the governor of Virginia. He concluded that the time had come to stop Teach once and for all. He spent weeks planning Blackbeard's capture. After

Blackbeard's ship was taken, a mate managed to escape and later joined my crew. I asked him to tell me the story of how his captain met his end. He told me that after everyone had left the gathering, Spotswood sent two sloops, commanded by Lieutenant Robert Maynard of the Royal Navy, to Ocracoke. After spotting the navy's sails, Teach and his crew realized that they were trapped. Only sandbars lay between them and the navy. By morning, the tide would rise, the sloops would glide over the submerged sandbars, and the attack on his ship would begin. I was told that the always-confident Teach didn't seem worried about the upcoming battle. His crew, however, was nervous. They stockpiled ammunition on deck and soaked blankets in water in preparation for putting out fires. They spread sand on the decks to soak up blood so others would not slip and lose their footing once the fighting started. In the morning, Teach didn't try to outrun the navy sloops. Instead, he waited at his ship's wheel. His crew was confused. Finally, when Maynard's sloops started moving toward the pirates, Teach began commanding his crew to set sail. They thought that he had gone mad and that he was steering the ship directly toward the beach, where they would surely crash. At the last minute, Teach maneuvered his ship through a narrow channel between the beach and a barely visible sandbar. While chasing his ship, the navy sloops crashed into the sandbar. Teach quickly turned the tables and ordered his gunners to open fire on the stranded sloops. Thundering explosions shook the waters. His ship then suddenly lurched backward and also became stuck on a sandbar."

"During the battle, one of the navy ships was completely destroyed. Maynard's sloop was also badly damaged and he ordered his men to throw everything over the side to lighten the vessel and remove it from the grasp of the sandbar. Losing the weight worked, and his ship floated free. Maynard's damaged sloop edged toward Teach's ship. Maynard ordered his men to hide below decks, with pistols and swords ready. Teach's men hurled grenades onto what appeared to be a deserted navy sloop, and easily boarded the ship. Suddenly, Maynard's men rushed the deck, firing pistols and wielding their cutlasses. Teach's crew was completely taken by surprise. With a pistol in one hand and cutlass in the other, Teach came face-to-face with Maynard. They both fired pistols. Teach missed. Maynard hit his mark. With a lead ball lodged in his chest, Teach still managed to swing his cutlass hard enough to snap Maynard's blade in two. Maynard drew back, but as Teach raised his arm to issue a finishing blow, a navy seaman slashed his throat from behind. Maynard's crew eventually won the battle and took over the ship and remaining crew. Teach's head was cut off and suspended from the bow of Maynard's sloop. His headless body was dumped overboard into the water. Two years have passed since I shook his hand, bade him farewell, and Godspeed the day before he died. "

"I am sure that most of us, as pirates, will be killed in battle either by explosion, pistol shot, or run through by saber, but I refuse to be humiliated in death by those that will end my life. I will not allow them to do with my carcass as they please. I can think of nothing worse than to end up with my dead body placed on display for others to gawk at and be eaten by birds and maggots. I have instructed my crew that if I am killed during battle, my body is to be weighted quickly and unceremoniously thrown into the drink."

"I conjured my ship's flag to represent our short and merry lives, a pirate on one side representing life and a skeleton on the other representing death. Both skeleton and pirate are joined in the center, holding an hourglass. It's only a matter of time before we meet our end. But I still believe, as I did after the first minute that I was made captain of my ship, it's better being a commander than a common man."

Jack interjects, "Out of all the flags flying on the seas, I have not seen one that has impressed me more than yours."

For some odd reason Roberts acts as if he doesn't know how to react to Jack's compliment. He could have simply acknowledged and thanked him, but instead, he smiles and without saying a word, flashes an awkward look at his quartermaster seated across the table from him.

Jack can't help but notice the awkward look and instantaneously becomes embroiled in a self-conscious argument with himself. Jack thinks, *Why did he react that way? Did my words sound strange? No, I simply complimented Roberts' flag! Why in bloody hell would he look at his quartermaster the way he did? Why am I feeing so embarrassed?*

Noticing the awkward moment he has created, Roberts quickly changes the subject. "Jack, I heard that your predecessor Charles Vane survived his marooning." Jack refocuses his attention to their conversation. If there is one man on this earth that he fears, it is Charles Vane. Jack had hoped that Vane and the others died after being cast adrift. Knowing that Vane has survived his ordeal, he fears that Vane will stop at nothing to find and kill him. He still has nightmares of Vane torturing his victims. As an officer under Vane's command, Jack was forced to participate in these heinous acts.

"After your crew relieved Vane of his command and cast him and others adrift, they had the good fortune to be spotted and rescued. As soon as they regained their strength, they managed to seize the ship that rescued them. Vane lost this ship to a reef during a violent storm. He and his surviving crew washed up on an uninhabited island. Eventually, another ship arrived, but unfortunately for Vane, a chap named Holford commanded this vessel. Captain Holford was a former buccaneer and acquaintance of Vane. Holford would not rescue Vane from the island. He told Vane that he would not trust him aboard his ship unless he was held as his prisoner. He knew that if he gave him access to his ship, Vane would surely plot to take it over. Vane was left on the island.

"Another ship soon arrived and, as none of the crew recognized Vane, he was allowed on board. Unfortunately for Vane, Captain Holford's ship met with this ship at sea and Holford was invited aboard to dine with the captain. While there, Holford saw Vane working on board, and he informed the captain who Vane was. The captain quickly relinquished Vane to Captain Holford, who locked him in his hold and promptly turned him over to the British authorities in Jamaica. The last I heard of Vane, he was awaiting trial. I am certain that he will be convicted of piracy and hanged. I have no doubt that his body will be pickled and also put on display for all to scorn."

"But now, captain, it is time to take our leave. The evening was truly magnificent and we do appreciate the hospitality that you and your crew have extended to us. However, it is time for much needed sleep before exploring Boston in the morn."

As the two groups of men leave the table and return to the ship's deck, Roberts pulls Jack aside to speak as the others continue to their boat. Roberts says in a subdued voice, "Jack, one last question before leaving ... I have heard rumors that you keep two women aboard your ship. Although I do not subscribe to breaking the pirate codes, the decisions you make aboard your ship as its commander are yours. I am, however, interested to know how they fare with hard labor and, at times, battle?"

"Captain Roberts, these women sail aboard this ship by the vote cast from my crew. They are on the account and given equal shares. They do not shy away from hard labor and are hellcats in battle. Mary Read can defeat most men I know with her sword. Anne Bonny is equally fierce in battle and can easily hold her own.

As the two talk, Jack sees a woman stepping from his quarters. He does not recognize that the made-up female approaching him is Anne until she is only a few feet away.

Anne makes a point to walk up to them. She has purposely shed her male clothing and replaced it with a corset and dress. In addition, she has groomed her hair, wearing makeup and a bonnet. Jack knows that Anne is doing this to embarrass and mock him for not including her to dine with the visiting men.

She interrupts their conversation and says, "Captain Roberts, forgive my interruption, before you leave us, I wanted to introduce myself. I am Anne Bonny. It was a pleasure to have you and your men aboard our ship. I trust that dinner was to your liking?" Before Roberts can respond, Anne continues, "I am one of two females aboard this ship who darns socks, and prepares delightful deserts for the crew. I also bed with Captain Rackham nightly in his quarters to make certain that his astounding sexual desires remain well fed." The only thing that hides Jack's embarrassed, reddened face is the dimly lit deck. Roberts releases an uncomfortable laugh, removes his hat, presents Anne with a gentleman's bow, and says, "My dear lady, the pleasure is all mine."

CHAPTER TWENTY-NINE

A FAIR TRADE

Jack directs his navigator to plot a course toward the northwestern coast of Cuba. Havana now within sight, *The Vanity* turns eastward. They hug the Cuban coastline, sailing 375 miles west and looking to prey upon small fishing vessels. Jack knows that attacking and capturing smaller ships means taking smaller prizes, but it also means much less risk. Fishing ships are built to catch fish, not fight battles. The essentials needed to operate fishing vessels can be judiciously stripped and traded for goods or sold to others while in port. A captured ship can be dismantled and sold for scrap or added to a captain's marauding fleet. As *The Vanity* sails around a rocky outcrop of land, Rackham suddenly hears the crewmember, perched in the crow's nest, shout, "Ship due east off the starboard bow." The stretch of land has hidden both ships from each other. As *The Vanity* makes its way around the strip of sand and volcanic rock, they find themselves practically on top of the fishing vessel. They have inadvertently snuck up on the smaller ship and are less than a hundred yards away. Jack sees the fishing vessel clearly, and sees that its crew is in a panicked state. He shouts an order to his crew, "Gentlemen, time to raise our flag and pounce on that ship."

When the crew of the fishing vessel sees Rackham's larger sloop closing in, they are completely taken by surprise. It's as if the ship appeared out of thin air. The Cuban crew sees of *The Vanity's* guns and the black flag as it is raised. The fishermen don't think twice, and they immediately raise a white flag to signal their surrender. Five of Jack's crew boards the smaller fishing sloop without a fight. At sword and gunpoint, the Cuban fishermen are brought aboard and herded into a corner on the ship's main deck. The captives are spoken to in their native Spanish language by one of Jack's deckhands. Jack tells the man to give the Cubans the option to go on the account, joining him as crewmembers, or be put ashore and marooned on an island. When presented with the two options, the fishermen suddenly realize that they are losing their ship. Jack has just taken away the means by which they are able to carry on their livelihood. They had hoped that if they gave up without a fight, the pirates might take their catch and possibly their nets and fishing tackle. The Cubans didn't expect them also to take their ship. As soon as they realize what is happening, they have a hard time controlling their anger and begin shouting profanity at Jack and his men: "Poyas!" ... "Qué Cabrón!" ..."Los cojones!" ... "Hijo de putaat!" Jack doesn't need to understand the Spanish language to know the types of words that are being thrown at him. He responds with one of the few Spanish words he knows.

"Alto!" The Cubans stop their verbal assault, turn back toward each other, and begin deliberating their choices. Jack leans against the ship's mast, while waiting for the Cubans' decision and makes small talk with several of his shipmates. The bantering between the Cubans intensifies. After waiting five minutes, Jack loses his patience and interrupts their heated conversation, "What say you Cubans? Join us or be marooned ... which will it be?" The Cubans stop talking, turn, and stare at Jack with blank faces, not understanding a word that he just said. Jack shakes his head in frustration and asks that his deckhand translate. One of the Cubans speaking for the group tells Jack's translator that given the choice of joining their pirate crew or being marooned on an island, they choose to be marooned. They believe that both choices will deliver the same fate—an untimely death. The fishermen have seen what the Spanish do to pirates when they are captured. After being captured, they are always tried, found guilty, and hanged by their necks. Some are even humiliated after death. The Spanish adopted one of the English methods to deter piracy. The dead bodies of executed pirates are covered with tar and displayed in metal cages called gibbets. A gibbet is a narrow, vertical iron cage that, with the help of several strategically located chains wrapped around a corpse's neck, torso, and lower legs, keeps the body upright in a standing position. The tar coating applied to a dead body creates a seal that limits the body's exposure to oxygen and other elements that promote the rapid decay of the flesh and substantially slows the natural decomposition process. A pirate's decaying body displayed in this manner serves as an effective warning to others who consider practicing piracy.

Jack is surprised by the fishermen's decision. "Very well, mate, tell the Cubans this ... marooned they shall be. As captain of this vessel, I will show them a mince of mercy and place them on an island north of our current position that is fairly close to merchant shipping lanes. If they are lucky, they should be found within two weeks by either a passing merchant ship or a Spanish warship charged with patrolling the waters that surround Cuba."

Jack believes that the fishermen will, in fact, be found by a passing merchant ship, but by the time they are found and report their ship was stolen, Jack, the stolen sloop, and *The Vanity* will be long gone. If the Spanish do decide to pursue them, they will not risk sailing too close to British-ruled Jamaica or having to engage in battle with British warships in order to recover a small fishing sloop. The British will unknowingly be protecting Jack and his crew, as they lie anchored at Port Royal.

The captured fishing sloop is less than a quarter the size of *The Vanity* and is in relatively good condition. If Jack decides to keep it, he will have two ships and the beginning of a flotilla. If he does choose to keep the sloop, several problems will need to be addressed. The ship's sails are worn and need replacing, and the ship's hull will need a good cleaning to remove the parasitic worms that attach themselves to the exterior of the hull and continually eat away at the wooden planks. If left unchecked, they will eventually cause irreparable damage.

Rackham tells his quartermaster, "Mister Corner, 'stead of unloading this sloop, I've made the decision that we will keep her and outfit her to carry out specialized raids on small coastal villages that lie on river banks and inlets. I want you to maroon these Cubans on one of the islands northwest of our current position. While you do this, I will take some men with me and sail around to the south side of the island to Media Luna. We will make the repairs she needs and rendezvous with you and *The Vanity* in three to five days in Port Royal. If we do not see you in six or more days, set sail to Media Luna and search for us."

Jack figures that the small vessel they've taken is from the north side of the island, most likely from Havana or a small outlying village nearby. He picks Media Luna because it's a small town on the opposite side of the island, far away from Havana. Although they will be fairly close to the larger city of Santiago de Cuba, he believes that they will be safe in a smaller town.

Jack picks six deckhands to help him sail the smaller boat through the treacherous waters. They finally reach the shallow waters of Media Luna and dock. Jack asks Ajani and a mate who speaks Spanish to join him. The three of them leave the sloop to search for new sails and try to find a buyer for the fishermen's tackle and nets. After asking local merchants, they find the canvases they need and are able to unload the tackle. As Jack and his men head back to the docks, they see one of their men running up the dirt road toward them. They meet in the middle of the road, and the winded shipmate pants, "Captain, two Spanish ships, one a warship the other a smaller sloop, have dropped anchor just outside the harbor." The four men make their way to the waterfront and board their sloop. Jack jumps from the dock onto the sloop. As his boots land on the deck, one of his men immediately shouts "Captain" and tosses Jack his spyglass. In a fluid motion, Jack extends the spyglass and places it to his eye. He brings the ships into focus. He spots what appears to be a ruckus taking place on the larger ship. A number of agitated men are pointing toward his position as they gather on its deck. He spots a Spanish naval officer looking directly at them through his own spyglass. Jack knows that he and the Spanish officer have locked eyes. Rather than pretend that they did not see each other, Jack decides to raise one hand and wave hello to the Spaniard as he continues looking at him through his spyglass. He can tell that the man has seen him due to his body language and decides to wave knowing that this action will likely confuse the officer. A friendly wave would not be an expected gesture coming from a trapped thief. Jack lowers his spyglass as he continues to peer at the Spanish warship. He raises the spyglass back to his eye to take another look. "Bloody hell, we cannot be this unlucky."

One of his men asks, "Captain, what do you see?"

"It's the men."

"Captain, which men?"

"The bloody Cubans."

"Do you mean the ..."

"Aye, the same bloody fishermen that we stole this sloop from and marooned. Surely, Mister Corner marooned them. Lads, they've spotted us and recognize their boat."

Jack's quartermaster had followed his orders to the letter. He and his men had sailed twenty-two miles from where they had stolen the fishing boat and marooned the men on a large, deserted island. Unfortunately for Jack, only ten hours after Mister Corner put the Cubans ashore and headed to Jamaica, a Spanish warship charged with patrolling the Cuban coast spotted and rescued them. The Spanish warship was returning to their base in Santiago de Cuba when they spotted the docked sloop fitting the description the Cuban fishermen had given them. It only took the Cuban fishermen a moment to confirm that the docked sloop was, indeed, theirs.

Jack tells his men, "Lads, your sight is true and there are two ships out there. The larger and closer ship to us is a Spanish warship, and it's a big bugger too! The other is an English sloop in tow, likely captured and now their prize.

"The Spanish ship is far too big and cannot get to us during low tide. This is why they dropped anchor at the harbor entrance and blocked our access to the sea. The tide will shift in their favor later this evening, allowing them to get close enough to engage us. Since it will be a moonless night, their captain will know it will be difficult to keep an eye on us. He won't want to risk our escape under the cover of darkness. They know we do not have cannons aboard this vessel, so they will look to take us with men and small arms to minimize the damage while attempting to reclaim the Cubans' ship. It's likely they will move on us during the night, having us trapped with our backs against land."

A concerned mate asks Jack, "Captain, how do you know that this is what the Spanish will do?"

"Because lad, it's what I would do if I were wearing conquistador boots."

Jack continues, "The Spanish will expect us to do one of two things: leave the vessel as it is docked during the night and escape inland, or try to make a run of it and attempt to elude them during the moonless night. They know it is likely that we will not choose the second option 'cause our odds of escaping by water will be slim. Even with a moonless night, they would easily be able to spot our sails as we passed. It looks as if we are trapped without a chance of sailing away. I've been tooling around a third option that I wager the Spanish will not be considering. This would see us sailing from this harbor to join *The Vanity* at Port Royal."

Another mate replies, "Captain, I don't understand. How can we sail if you just told us that we are trapped with no chance of escaping by water?"

Jack hands the confused shipmate his spyglass and says, "Lad, Take a look at those two ships and tell me what you see."

"Aye, captain," as the man puts the lens close to one eye and closes his other.

Jack inquires, "All right, what do you see?"

"I see two ships, one a larger gun ship and the smaller captured English sloop."

"Aye mate, I believe that I am taking a fancy to that English sloop. I think that we shall trade this small Cuban sloop for something more grand and English. What say you?" The men look at each other and they all begin to laugh. Jack joins in the laughter.

"We will have to act quickly if we are to have a chance to carry out my plan. First, I need two men to secure three ten-pound powder kegs and forty feet of slow-burning fuse. Ajani and I will pay a local to serve as the lighter of the fireworks show we will stage for our Spanish friends this evening. I need the rest of you to secure a longboat and pay a good fee to make certain the boat is brought out to the edge of the harbor. It must be hidden from the Spaniards' sight. Make sure they conceal the boat with palms and brush so it is not to be noticed. They need to half-bury a rum bottle in the sand two hundred paces east of the hidden boat. This will make it easier for us to find."

That afternoon, Jack's men place the three powder kegs on the shoreline directly behind the Cuban's sloop. They separate the kegs with enough distance to ensure that when the first one explodes it will not ignite the others. They also build a horseshoe-shaped stack of stones around each of the kegs, leaving the open end facing the water. The stone barrier around each keg will further ensure that the other kegs will not explode when the first keg ignites. They attach three lengths of fuse to the kegs, each length two feet longer than its neighbor, ensuring that the kegs explode in succession. Having the sloop between the explosions and the Spanish warship will give the impression, from a distance that the sloop is exploding. Jack pays a local boy to light the three fuses at exactly eight o'clock, after the tide begins to rise.

Jack and his men load their belongings and secure them onto mules. They grab their weapons and begin their trek across land to reach the area where the longboat is hidden. At sunset, they reach the shoreline about a half-mile away from where the Spanish warship is anchored. The men walk on the sandy shoreline and locate the half-buried rum bottle. Jack takes two hundred paces west and points toward the tree line where the Cuban jungle meets the beach. His men begin combing through the tangled, overgrown bushes and vines finally coming across the well-hidden boat.

Jack says, "Mates, gather round so that I can tell you how I see taking that ship. The tide should have started changing over an hour ago. I reckon the Spanish will raise their anchor and begin closing on the Cubans' sloop at close to eight o'clock. The powder kegs should begin to blow at about this time. The explosions will keep the warship on guard, focused on the shoreline. The English sloop will remain anchored where it is now. The Spaniards charged with guarding the prize will also be focused on the shore and the explosions.

While they gawk, we will approach this ship from behind and from the opposite direction of the action. Ajani will board the ship by climbing the anchor chain, and he will lower a rope ladder that will bring the rest of us aboard. We do not know the number of men that guard the sloop, but I reckon that there should not be more men than we have. Once aboard, we will split into two groups. You four in one, and Samuel, you, me, and Ajani will make up the second. No pistols are to be fired during our attack. We must do-away with the guards quickly and silently. We cannot allow them to fire a shot to alert the warship. If alerted, they will give chase. Even though our sloop will be swifter than the warship, we won't be able to outrun their guns."

It is nearly eight o'clock. Jack and his men wait patiently in their longboat, close to the shoreline and out of sight. Eight o'clock comes and goes and Jack becomes apprehensive. The Spanish warship has not shown any sign of sailing toward the abandoned Cuban fishing sloop, and the explosions have not happened.

Jack whispers to his men, "Surely the young lad we paid to light our fuses would not have taken our money and run. He would—" Jack abruptly interrupts himself in midsentence as he hears the voices of two men emerge from the direction of the Spanish warship. Jack places his index finger to his lips. If they can hear the Spaniards, then the Spaniards can surely hear them. They remain as still as possible while the ocean's soft rolling swells raise and lower their boat in a gentle and calming motion. They strain their eyes as they gaze toward the warship to catch a glimpse of what's happening. They hear several more voices and see flickers of light begin to illuminate portions of the ship's deck. A bouncing light begins to move across the deck, caused by a lantern being carried by a deckhand as he and another man walk toward the ship's anchor. Jack notices that their longboat has drifted faster and much further than he expected. If they drift any closer to the ship, even the darkness will not conceal their presence. The current continues to move them closer, as the voices of the Spanish become louder and clearer. They are so close to the warship that they can see the pattern on one of the deckhands' shirts. The tension aboard the longboat peaks as it drifts alongside the bow of the warship and moves unnoticed behind the Spaniards' captured British sloop. Jack nods his head and directs his men's attention to extend their arms to prevent their boat from colliding with the side of the British sloop. Now, behind the sloop, they are out of the warship's sight. As long as the Spaniards tasked with guarding the sloop do not notice them, they will be in a perfect position to carry out their plan.

The loud and unmistakable clattering of the warship's heavy anchor chain being raised begins to fill the air and can be heard for miles as the sound reflects off the water's surface.

Jack hears orders being given to the crew, and the sails are hoisted into position. The warship is finally preparing to sail toward the shoreline and the abandoned fishing sloop.

The warship moves very slowly, as it begins to gain

momentum. Five minutes pass, before a brilliant flash lights up the bay as the first ten-pound black powder keg explodes. With the Spaniards' full attention now on the shoreline, it's time for Ajani to board the English sloop. The others maneuver the boat closer. Ajani secures a tightly wrapped bundle of spears to his back, leans forward, grabs the large chain, and pulls himself upward, wrapping his legs around the anchor chain to steady himself. Within minutes, Ajani reaches the deck of the ship. He looks, sees no one, and pulls himself over the side onto the ship's deck. He quickly pulls a rope ladder from the pack on his back, secures it, and lowers it over the side of the ship to where Jack and the others wait. Each man quickly climbs aboard. They leave most of their gear and belongings on the longboat until they secure the English vessel. Once all are onboard, the first group moves to the left side of the ship while Jack and his move to the right. At this moment, the second powder keg explodes, momentarily lighting up the night sky. Jack and his men pause their advance for a brief second, until the darkness covers them again. As Jack and his men move closer to the middle of the ship, they see three Spanish guards watching the flames burning on the shore. Jack and his men approach the guards from behind. He quietly gets within a few feet of the closest guard, draws a ten-inch blade from its sheath and lunges toward his unsuspecting victim, covers the Spaniard's mouth with his left hand as he presses his knife's blade hard against the man's neck, slicing a three-inch deep wound across the length of the Spaniard's neck, severing his carotid artery and windpipe. The two guards standing by the side of the ship closest to the shore don't hear a thing. Jack and his men begin to move on them when a muffled yell is heard. Both guards take a defensive posture and one calls out to his comrades, "¿Eduardo ... Augusto, es usted aceptable? ¿Dónde está usted?" After hearing no response, the guard strains his eyes in an attempt to see any movement through the darkness. The other guard unknowingly turns his head toward Jack and his men. Taken completely by surprise, his eyes grow as large as saucers as he sees three attackers only feet from him. Jack begins to run toward the guard, as one of Ajani's spears flies over Jack's shoulder and slams into the guard's chest, causing him to fall backward against the side of the ship. The other guard turns quickly, raising his musket toward Jack. Jack grabs the gun's barrel and pushes it to the side, pulls his cutlass from its sheath, and raises it above his head. The guard yells, "¡Parada!" Before Jack is able to strike, Ajani jumps in front of Jack and plunges another of his spears into the guard's heart. The guard lets out a gasp, grabs the shaft of the spear, and falls limp to the ground. The third and final powder keg explodes, as Jack, Ajani, and Samuel move cautiously across the deck toward the middle of the ship to see how the other group fared. Jack sees three men lying motionless. He hears a disembodied voice come from a dark corner, "Captain!"

"Aye, show yourself." His men appear from the darkness. Jack asks, "All still with us? How many were killed?"

"We put down four Spaniards."

"Excellent! Gentlemen, I want this ship sailing within

minutes, before that warship heads back our way. I will steer our prize."

The seven-man crew raises the ship's sails, weighs anchor, and quietly slips away. As the sloop gains speed and distance, Jack looks back and sees only a small yellow-orange glow on shore. He throws up his arms, looks into the dark sky, and yells out to his men, "A fair trade it was! Men, maybe it's just me, but it seems that victory has a sweeter taste at night!"

Jack turns the ship's wheel southward, on a course toward Port Royal. He has not slept in over forty-two hours, but he is not tired. What happened less than one hour ago still has him buzzing. He begins to sing a shanty and his six mates join in. All sing loudly.

"Oh, blow the man down, bullies, blow the man down ..."

"Way, aye blow the man down ..."

"Oh, blow the man down, bullies, blow him away ..."

"Give me some time to blow the man down ..."

"As I was a walking down Paradise Street ..."

"A pretty young damsel I chanced for to meet ..."

"Give me some time to blow the man down!"

As the ship sails further into the night, the sound of the men singing fades and eventually is drowned out by the ambient sounds of the sea.

A day and a half later, as Jack and his new English sloop approach Port Royal, he says, "Samuel, come steer our ship while I search for *The Vanity*." Jack looks through his spyglass toward the harbor, and scans the anchored ships. He quickly spots his ship, anchored in Kingston Bay. He lowers the spyglass and smiles.

Chapter Thirty

The Strong Spaniard

While aboard the ship, Anne does not wear women's clothes. Skirts and corsets are not practical for the daily duties she performs aboard the ship. Mary has not been seen in a dress since the brief time she was married, and has spent the rest of her life disguised as a male. Instead, Anne and Mary wear clothes similar to the male crew. All aboard wear trousers and loosely fitting shirts. Most wear scarves wrapped around their heads to keep their hair from becoming a nuisance when doing their work. Others wear hats to keep the intense sun from baking their brains during the day.

After Mary's true identity was revealed, all deception was abandoned. The relationship between Anne and Mary grows, and they become very close. Being the only females aboard a ship filled with men creates a bond that the two have not experienced their whole lives. Anne says to Mary, "For God's sake, I cannot believe that I thought you to be such a handsome young warrior. To think that I was so determined to get a good rogering from you." The thought causes the two to begin laughing uncontrollably. They laugh even more as they see the confused faces of passing shipmates trying to determine what is so amusing.

Jack and his crew have now sailed back up and down the coast of America. The crew has had little luck finding ships to engage, so Jack resets a course to sail off the northwestern coast of Jamaica. Yells of "ship ahoy!" ring out, causing Anne and Mary to jump to their feet. They begin scanning the horizon toward the direction the lookout is pointing.

Mary puts her hand to her forehead to block the sun from her eyes and says, "Anne, I see the ship."

Anne asks, "Where? I don't see it."

"Straight out off port side."

Jack and the quartermaster are quick to appear on the scene. Looking at the ship through his spyglass. Jack tells him, "She's Spanish, an older-style merchant ship with no escorts."

The quartermaster replies, "Captain, shall we see what she holds?"

"Aye, raise our flag and inform the master gunner and crew to prepare to engage that ship."

As *The Vanity* sails closer to the Spanish merchant ship, Mary begins loading her pistols and checking to make sure that she's well stocked with ammunition. She tells Anne, "The Spanish are used to battle. They are a hardened lot, having been fighting wars for hundreds of years. Even though this is a merchant ship, I would wager that they will be ready for us and won't back down. This will be your first time in battle. I want you to promise me that you will focus and remember all you've learned during your training, and most of all, mind your temper."

Mary begins to talk to Anne in a calming voice. "Just as the British have spent centuries training armies and fighting wars to conquer as much of the world as they can, so have the Spanish and French. Aside from their languages, uniforms and flags, the British, Spanish, and French empires are very much alike. Their kings, queens, ships, guns, and military tactics are practically identical. The way I see it, the only difference between them are their military officers. During my time in the military, I have noticed that the commanders who keep their wits about them during times of battle are the commanders who win victories and reap the greatest rewards."

Mary goes on, "It never fails before any battle; the thought of one of my experiences enters my mind. As a mercenary, I began my military experience as a British foot soldier fighting against the French. I later joined a horse regiment during the Nine Years War. I witnessed many men rush headlong into battle, determined to kill all in sight only to find themselves one of many who watched their own souls leave their bodies. Six months after joining the horse regiment, our First

Lieutenant received a dispatch informing him that a French artillery regiment had taken position atop a strategically located hill overlooking the terrain for miles. Our lieutenant sent word of our orders to attack the enemy, capture the position, and do away with the French troops. The captain ordered the raid to take place under the cover of darkness, in hopes of taking the French by surprise. We broke camp and headed toward the French stronghold. I was among six troops ordered to serve as an advanced scouting party to observe and assess the enemy's strength and position. The regiment would hold back and wait for our information before finalizing plans and moving forward with the assault.

"Our scouting party rode hard toward the French position, planning to dismount our horses a mile from the French and approach them on foot. As we crossed a high grass meadow, flashes of light illuminated the far end of the field, followed by the unmistakable sounds of cannon fire.

"The violent sound of cannonballs ripping through the air was followed by four explosions around us—one forty yards behind us and another three thirty yards behind us. My horse panicked, reared onto his hind legs, and threw me into the field. The French fired a second salvo. With my face in the dirt, explosions were happening all around me. I heard a loud cry as one of our horses was hit with flying shrapnel. Then all went silent. Clouds of smoke created by the explosions were rising slowly from the tall grass. I yelled out to my comrades and began crawling on my hands and knees toward where I believed them to be. I suddenly found myself wet and covered with mud. I thought that I had crawled into a small stream. I then noticed that the water appeared black on the grass around me and covered my hands and uniform. You see, at night under the moonlight, blood appears to be black. I realized that I was not crawling in a stream of water and mud, but in a pond of blood. I quickened my pace and came across one of our fallen horses. The dying animal was panting heavily as it was taking its last breaths of life. I began calling the names in my troop. Three answered. I told them to keep low, to stay below the level of the tall grass, and to work their way to the side of the field where a line of trees would protect us."

Anne remains motionless as she marvels at Mary's story.

"Within minutes, all of us made it to the trees. The French had sent a patrol into the meadow to search for us. We could clearly see and hear them as they approached what was left of the bodies of our two fallen comrades. Between the four of us, we had three sabers, two muskets, and two pistols. With our sergeant lying dead in the field, we had no leadership. The remaining men were young and inexperienced. Without a thought, I took control and told them that we were to complete our mission and assess the strength of the French encampment. I had them follow me to approach the camp from behind. We only spotted six troops and four cannons. I quickly realized that we had stumbled upon an undetected French artillery unit and not the larger force we were sent to find. I ordered the men to fix their bayonets, to kill silently and shoot only if absolutely necessary. I spotted one lone

Frenchy smoking a pipe and focusing on the patrol still searching for us in the meadow. I was able to approach him from behind, and when I was within a few feet of him, I plunged a dagger into his back. I covered his mouth with my other hand to stop him from alerting the other French troops. I quickly removed his jacket and disguised myself. I also wore his hat and I even smoked his pipe. I walked freely just outside the dim light cast by their lanterns. I heard one of the French troops shouting questions out to the patrol. "Les voyez-vous? Combien? Y a-t-il des survivants?" As the French were still searching in the field, I quietly ordered my men to attack. Using the element of surprise, we used our bayonets and sabers to cut them down. We then turned the cannons against those still in the field and tore them to shreds."

"Mary, if I could only have been by your side, it would have been glorious."

"Glorious? I reckon recounting my experience as a story may glorify the actions we took, but it was far from glorious. It was bloody serious. We lost two good men and all of us could have died in the meadow that night. We survived because I was able to keep my wits about me, controlling my fear, my hatred for the enemy and my thoughts of revenge. I carefully assessed the situation and commanded what needed to be done. The next morning I felt myself fortunate to be alive."

As they gain on the Spanish ship, Jack sees them raise a white flag to signal their surrender. Jack scoffs, "I'll be damned. They decided not to fight and are surrendering their ship to us." Because Jack is not the most trusting soul, he decides to maneuver his ship in a half circle around to approach the Spanish vessel from behind. *The Vanity* finishes its maneuver and slowly moves beside the ship so that the two are parallel. As they advance to less than twenty feet away from the Spanish, Jack sees the crew moving about the deck. He notices that their movements seem odd. As they draw even closer, he notices that the Spaniards have scattered crows' feet on the deck of their ship. The Spanish are known for using these razor sharp barbs to inflict nasty wounds upon barefooted pirates and privateers who unsuspectingly jump onto the deck of their ships. Jack has seen barefoot men land on crows' feet before. Their feet are sliced, they lose toes, and they always fall, making them easy targets. A thought suddenly hits Jack. The Spanish are not intending to surrender. There's only one reason why they would have scattered crows' feet about their deck. The Spanish plan to draw his crew aboard and launch a surprise attack. He doesn't have a second to warn his crew before he hears a loud single word yelled from the Spanish ship: "Ataque!"

Jack sees every Spaniard on the ship sprinting toward him and his crew. He looks back and yells to his crew, "It's a trick, mates!" As Jack turns back toward the Spanish ship, he is instantly hit in the chest by a flying grappling hook. The blunt force of the twenty-pound iron hook knocks him off balance and he falls backward onto the deck.

With the wind knocked out of him, he looks to see his men scrambling for their weapons as guns are fired all around them. Jack sees a stream of additional grappling hooks fly over the heads of his men and the tines of the hooks dig deeply into the wooden planks of *The Vanity*. He cannot believe that the Spanish have turned the tables and are preparing to board. He pauses for a second to regain his composure. Jack looks up to see where Anne is and spots her heading toward him. He hears Anne yell, "Jack!" She falls to one knee beside him and grabs a handful of his shirt. He looks at Anne and says, "Only knocked off my feet. Stay close by my side." Anne releases his shirt, lets out a banshee scream, and lunges toward the Spanish ship

As Jack gets back to his feet, he yells to his men, "Slaughter them all!" With this order, Jack unleashes the fury of his crew. Before the order was given, his men were fighting chaotically. Once they hear Jack's thundering voice, they organize a cohesive attack and swarm aboard the Spanish vessel. Anne sees Mary and the others jump from *The Vanity* to the deck of the Spanish ship, and follows.

Anne jumps onto the side of the ship. She looks at the vicious battle that is taking place aboard the Spaniards' deck. Through the sound of guns firing, exploding grenades and men yelling, she leaps from *The Vanity* to the Spanish deck. She sees Mary run a Spaniard through with her sword before disappearing in a cloud of smoke. Her mind is racing. Every nerve ending in her body is telling her to flee the scene for safety, but she disregards her instincts and heads to engage the closest enemy. The man she chooses to fight sees her coming and turns to face her. Anne remembers what Mary told her before the battle about keeping her wits and outthinking her enemy.

She lets out an insane scream and swings her sword. As a defensive move, the Spaniard swings his sword in an upward motion to meet Anne's. In a flash, he directs his sword back toward Anne in a roundhouse motion. Anne puts her sword out in front of her as their weapons collide. The force of the Spaniard's blow is so great that it causes her arm instantly to go numb.

The Spaniard uses his free arm to throw a sharp jab that connects squarely against Anne's nose. Her head snaps backward and she stumbles, taking two awkward steps backward as blood begins to pour from her nose.

She quickly assesses the man she is fighting and realizes that he is a large, strong man. She is completely physically outmatched. With a crazed look in his eyes, the Spaniard smiles, cuts the air with one swift swing of his sword and says, "¡Venido a mí!" As the Spaniard steps toward Anne, he is struck in the shoulder by a musket ball and is thrown off balance. Anne sees the opportunity, races toward him, swings her sword, and slashes his bicep, leaving a gaping wound. The two now stand face-to-face, Anne tells the Spaniard, "Your life is over."

The Spaniard replies, "¡Todavía me no acaban!" He pushes Anne with such force that she leaves her feet, flying backward, slamming hard onto the ship's deck. Her sword is knocked from her hand and slides away across the deck. She rolls over onto her stomach and realizes that she cannot breathe. The force from landing hard onto the wooden planks has knocked the air from her lungs. In a panic, she crawls away, struggling to regain her breath and her weapon. She senses the Spaniard is close behind.

As she reaches her sword, she turns back to see the goliath standing over her, readying his final blow. Anne suddenly realizes that she is finished. With no options, she faces the man who will end her life and lets out a defiant scream. Anne sees the Spaniard's body jerk as he winces. She turns her head and sees Ajani pulling his pistol back as he rushes off to engage another. The musket ball fired by Ajani enters the side of the Spaniard's torso, shattering a rib and tearing through vital organs. The impact causes him to stumble awkwardly toward Anne. Anne pushes her sword into the Spaniard. His eyes suddenly widen, he coughs up blood and falls on top of her. She rolls the dead Spaniard off, pulls her sword from his body, and moves to join her shipmates.

The battle lasts only twenty minutes. When it finally ends, Jack and his crew take control of the Spanish ship. Eight of Jack's crewmembers and twenty-two of the Spanish are killed. The remaining wounded and those who surrendered are cast adrift to die. Before scuttling the Spanish ship, he instructs his crew to transfer all valuables to *The Vanity*.

That evening, Anne tells Mary, "During our fight, I engaged a hulk of a man. I did all I could to remember what you told me. As I joined the battle, I tried to contain my emotions, but I could not. From the moment I engaged the

Spaniard, I made critical mistakes. The Spaniard used my mistakes against me to gain an upper hand. I found myself overmatched, and, in a matter of seconds, I was lying on my back realizing that I was about to die. As the Spaniard stood over me, he was fired upon and struck in his side. This gave me a chance to run the bastard through. It was Ajani who shot the Spaniard. If not for him, I would be dead."

Anne spots Ajani and walks over to him. Ajani, your true aim saved me from feeling a Spanish cutlass run me through. I will be forever grateful to you. You are my savior." Anne leans her body forward and extends herself, standing on the tips of her toes, to kiss Ajani's cheek. Ajani smiles, and with his very limited knowledge of the English language, responds "Anne, safe ... Blessed God."

While sailing the high seas, Anne spends time with Ajani. Even though Ajani does not speak or understand the English language very well, the two learn to communicate, and create a special bond. While at sea, Anne realizes that Ajani has taken a liking to her. He watches over her during times of battle and protects her from harm, as an older brother would protect his younger sister.

CHAPTER THIRTY-ONE

CONFESSIONS

After Anne and Jack dine with the crew on a typical fare of salted beef, beans, and biscuits, they retire to his quarters. While lying in bed, Anne turns to Jack and asks, "Have you ever feared for your life?"

Jack takes a moment to think and responds, "Annie, just between the two of us, I will tell you yes. I have feared for my life many times. However, if any man outside this cabin were to ask me the same question I would say to them that I have not feared one thing in my life since leaving my mother's womb. In our profession, fear is looked upon as a sign of weakness. If you show fear, you will not go far."

Jack loves Anne deeply, but because of her past, he does not trust her unconditionally. In the short amount of time they have been together, Jack has seen her manipulate unsuspecting people and situations to get what she wants. He knows that if Anne wants something badly enough, she will do whatever it takes to lay claim to her prize. For a moment, Jack almost confesses his biggest fear to Anne: that the pressures of being a captain are far greater than he imagined and that he is in constant fear of losing his command to a crew's vote or mutiny. He decides to keep this thought only to himself. Instead, Jack tells her of his fears that he knows if repeated, will not have a possibility of haunting him later.

Anne moves her body closer to Jack and lays her head upon his chest, "So tell me captain, what else do you fear? Do you fear me?"

"Ha, fear you? Now why would I fear a flower such as yourself, even though you are often more of an impetuous tiger lily than a delicate rose? I will tell you of things I have feared throughout my life. As a child, I feared rats and the creatures of the deep. I often heard stories about rats chewing the fingers off senseless drunks that would drink, pass out, and wake up to find that a swarm of rats had smelt the scent of dinner on his fingers and eaten them down to nubs. When I was older, I realized that my mother told me this story in order to keep me from falling in love with hard drink. I also recall my father showing sketches of monsters of the sea and telling me tales of how these monsters would rise from the ocean depths to attack ships, killing all aboard. When I was still young, I also feared my father's anger. Just the sound of him raising his deep voice was enough to send me for shelter under my bed. When I was a young man, I feared loving any one woman. I would not allow the thought to enter into my mind. I thought that if I were to settle on a specific woman, I would surely not lead the life I set off to live. For a long time, I thought it would be best to love all women. You, my dear, are my only exception."

"Jack, hearing you speak of your feelings of me sends a warm feeling through my soul. You have taught me the true meaning of love." Anne continues asking more probing questions. "When was the last time you cried?"

Jack is confused about why Anne is asking him such deeply personal questions. Since she has never talked to Jack this way, he is suspicious about what her true intentions are.

Jack has seen her manipulate many of his crewmembers, and he realizes that she has done the same to him on several occasions. After concluding that there is no ulterior motive to her questions, he takes the opportunity to share more about his past. "When I was twelve years old, my mother sat me down at our kitchen table and told me that my father was never going to return. He had been killed while being robbed along a street in London. I cried myself to sleep for weeks."

"Jack, I am so sorry. Having this happen to you at such a young age must have been hard on you."

"Aye Lass, It was hard to muster through. My father has been gone for half my life and I still mourn his death. I have thoughts of him daily. I sometimes find myself looking skyward to the clouds and wonder if he watches me from above."

"Do you ever see him? Do you believe in God?"

"Annie, I only see him in my thoughts and when I dream. I would like to believe there is a good and merciful God that watches over us all. If there is a God, I know that he has shown me one sign of his existence. He has brought you to me. I have also seen men do unspeakable things to each other, and if God was watching, he did not lift a finger to stop their suffering. I myself have killed men and have cursed the Lord's name more times than I can count. I do know that the line that divides good and evil is a thin and blurred line. Take me for an example. I consider myself to be a fair man, a man of good nature. Others that consider themselves virtuous and champions of God would consider me a scourge, a man without morals, a murderous fiend whose soul will surely burn in hell. I also believe that if there is a God, then there must also be a devil, and with the countless sins I have committed, my soul will surely go to him. I do not know, Anne; I reckon this mystery will resolve itself as I am hanged, run through, or wind up lucky enough to die an old man.

"Enough about me, let's talk about you. Tell me about your feelings after experiencing your first taste of battle with the Spaniards."

"It was the most exhilarating and fearful experience of my life. My heart raced as I jumped from *The Vanity* to the deck of the Spanish ship. I found that I had no time to think about my emotions as I began fighting the Spaniard who nearly ended my life. After the battle, my mind and body were no good to me. All I wanted to do was to fall into a deep sleep. The next day I was lying in bed and began to cry uncontrollably. When you later entered the cabin, I pretended to be asleep. I did not want to talk to you or anyone else, nor did I sleep the entire night. I have no understanding of why I cried. I had no feelings for the man I killed, nor for our crewmates that were lost during the battle."

"Lass, I have known grown men to have the emotions you speak of. There is something that happens to a person's mind after experiencing the violence and carnage of their first battle. I hear that it is common for one to cry after killing their first human. I think it best that you not worry yourself thinking about why you felt the way you did. Allow it to pass.

"We've become close, but, in many ways, I still don't feel I know a lot about you. In other ways, I feel I know everything. Tell me of your father, your mother and your childhood in Charles Towne."

"I look back at my life in Charles Towne and have many fond memories. When I was a young child, I did not realize how fortunate I was to lead a life of comfort. The only price I had to pay was to wake each morning and experience the life I was given. As I grew older, I realized that leading this life of comfort came with a price. All that surrounded me, all that I experienced, was provided and controlled by my father. When I was very young, I worshiped him. He was tall, strong in body and mind. I was obedient and did as I was told, without question. As I grew older, I realized that he was fueled by the need to dominate and control. This included both my mother and me. After hearing him berate her on numerous occasions, I began to question all that he was. Not knowing how to deal with these situations, I quietly ignored them. Then one day I'd had enough and told him to leave her be. Because of my outburst and belligerent display of disrespect, my father treated me as if I was a piece of spoiled meat for nearly a year. I grew to despise him. After this incident, my mother became withdrawn. She never thanked me for standing up for her. She also turned a blind-eye toward my father's poor treatment of me. Although I dearly loved her, I never understood why she would never fight back. Why was she subservient to that bastard? I never fully appreciated or realized how much she meant to me until after she was gone. After she died, I was put in charge of running the daily duties of my father's estate. I felt that I had inherited the role of being the head house servant for my father. My entire perspective on life changed. Running the affairs of his estate were both demanding and boring. Daily routines were forced upon me. I wanted more, and I wanted a way out. When I first met James, I realized that he was the answer. I also knew that James stood for everything that my father despised in a man. Looking back, James served two purposes for me. He provided a way to rebel against my father's dominance, and he provided my path to independence.

The life that I have chosen, our relationship and sailing the seas as a pirate, satisfies me. It has its own hardships, but the adventure and freedom it has brought to me cannot be replaced."

Jack releases a loud and exaggerated yawn, "Aye lass ...

the way I see it is that if we are put on this earth to live only one life, then should we not take all we can?"

"Jack, I know that this may sound odd coming from me, but after we have had our fill of sailing the seas, I would like to find a quiet corner somewhere near the ocean and settle."

CHAPTER THIRTY-TWO

THE HUNT

Jack anchors his ship in a secluded cove to spend a few days caring for his wounded crew. He issues orders for his men to take turns spending time doing as they wish on the Jamaican shore. He wants them to step away from the ship for a short while to clear their heads of what they have just gone through. Although they have been victorious and captured the Spanish merchant ship, they have paid a heavy price.

"Annie, we all are battered and bruised. Looking back on what has happened, I believe the Spaniards had a sound strategy. The captain knew that his ship was grossly overmatched. They had no other choice than to break the code of the sea by raising their white flag in order to trick us into thinking that they had surrendered in an attempt to save their ship and its cargo. By raising their white flag, they would not draw our cannon fire. By duping us, they would allow us to pull alongside their ship and bring the fight to us. Their plan might've worked if our crew was not so experienced in battle. Just as I have sent our men ashore to clear their heads, so must we. You and I will go ashore for some target practice. Have you ever hunted wild pigs?"

"Jack, I can honestly say that I have not, nor any other animal."

"Well, I can tell you that when cooked over a spit, they are delicious creatures. The only problem with them is that they can be dangerous, nasty critters. They also have unpredictable tempers, kind of like you, Annie."

The two set out for shore and into the Jamaican jungle to search for game. Before they leave, Jack makes sure they both have loaded pistols and a musket. Jack uses a machete to cut through the heavy growth. He wants to get closer to the bank of the river that flows into the sea, for he knows that where there is fresh water, there is typically wild game. The two finally make it to a clearing close to the riverbank. They sit patiently behind a thicket of dense ferns. Jack quietly whispers, "Annie, you need to know a few things about these creatures. When being hunted, if a sow feels that her youngsters are threatened, or if she finds herself cornered, she becomes a ferocious animal. Sows often grow to well over three hundred pounds and when they charge they aim to kill. If we come across one of these beasts, our aim must be true."

"The sow's counterpart, the "boar," is smaller but equally ferocious. They sport large tooth-like tusks, which can be lethal. If your aim is off and you miss, you won't have time to reload. The best thing for you to do is quickly climb the nearest tree. We should have luck here. The pigs become more active at dusk and into the night foraging for food." Jack points to the clearing. "That there would be a game trail. The path is cleared by a steady flow of game coming from other areas of the jungle to drink from this river. All is in our favor—fresh water, approaching darkness, evidence of game frequenting this area, and a clearing providing us with a place to take aim and kill the bloody oinkers."

Jack and Anne sit until dusk. Suddenly, they begin to hear the sound of rustling leaves, branches breaking and pigs snorting. Jack puts his index finger to his lips and blows, "shhhh ..." He whispers quietly, "The pigs are rooting the ground. They push dirt, leaves, and small branches aside with their snouts while searching for food." The animals come into view. One large sow, followed by three smaller pigs, appears less than thirty yards from where Anne and Jack are hiding.

Jack motions for Anne to stand slowly and take aim. Suddenly gunshots are heard in the near distance, agitating the four pigs. Jack motions for Anne to stay still, but she decides to take aim and shoot anyway. She slowly raises her musket, takes aim and squeezes the trigger. The hammer slams down on top of the flint, igniting the flintlock's gunpowder. The lead ball explodes from the end of the barrel. The gun's sudden explosion causes the pigs to jump in unison. Anne misses the sow. The sow sees the two of them, lets out a loud squeal and charges her instantly. Anne panics, drops her musket, and screams as she turns and begins running down the path from which they had come. Jack stays calm, points his musket, fires, and misses. He turns and begins to sprint down the same path as Anne. As he is running, he yells, "Damn! Damn! Damn! Annie, climb that tree!" The sow gains on Jack and Anne. They latch onto the nearest tree trunks and shimmy their bodies upward as fast as they can. Both Jack and Anne are out of breath and their skin is scratched and scuffed from scraping against the coarse tree bark, but laugh as they cling tightly to the trees.

The sow and the piglets circle beneath them. Laughing, Jack takes one of his pistols from his belt, aims and fires. The sow jumps in place, snorts and falls dead. The two laugh uncontrollably. Anne yells, "Jack, kill the others before they get away!" Anne and Jack return from their hunt with the sow and two of the piglets.

Chapter Thirty-Three

The Duel

As Jack and Anne near the ship, they see a group of four men carrying muskets from the jungle. Jack says to Anne, "It looks like some of the men had the same idea as we did. They must've been hunting close by and are responsible for the shots we heard earlier." As the men draw nearer, Jack notices that they seem agitated and appear to be arguing with each other. Within fifty yards, he recognizes two of them: Thomas Earl yelling at Robert Hempstead. Hempstead pushes Earl and the two begin throwing punches, fall to the sand, and wrestle each other on the shore. Jack hears the other two men cheering the fight on. It is common knowledge that Hampstead is a somewhat nasty character. Jack and many of his crew have recognized him as one of the few men who have a true thirst for killing. Jack drops the leg of the sow that he has been dragging back to the ship and walks over to the fighting men as Anne follows. "All right lads, that would be enough." Earl stops fighting immediately when he hears the captain's voice. Hampstead also stops, but decides to get in one last cheap shot by giving Earl a sharp jab to his ribs.

When he first became captain of *The Vanity*, Jack memorized the eleven rules referred to, by most, as the "Pirate Code." With this situation presenting itself, Jack sees an opportunity to invoke number eight of the code. "Lads, given what I have witnessed, I feel it my duty as your captain to remind you of rule number eight of the pirate code. ... *None shall strike another on board the ship, but every man's quarrel shall be ended on shore by sword or pistol.* At the command from the quartermaster, each man, being previously placed back-to-back, shall turn and fire immediately. If any man does not fire, the quartermaster shall knock the piece out of his hand. If both miss their aim, they shall take to their cutlasses. He that draws first blood shall be declared the victor." After reciting the rule, Jack goes on to say, "Since your squabble was not aboard the ship, but on land, no rules have been broken. However, I remind you of this so as to not bring your fighting aboard my ship. We fight others for gain and not against ourselves in anger."

Hempstead responds by saying, "Aye, captain, I remember number eight as well as number six. Captain Rackham, you do remember rule six, do you not? *No woman is to be allowed to sail aboard a ship. If any man shall be found seducing any woman on board the ship or carrying her to sea in disguise, he shall suffer death.*" As Hampstead finishes, he looks beyond Jack at Anne. She folds her arms and curls her lip in disgust. Hampstead's insubordination and obvious lack of respect for Jack's authority rattle him. He hasn't particularly cared for Hampstead up to this point and has tolerated him only because he's a hard-working man and a decent fighter. This situation's disrespect causes Jack to consider that it would not be a bad thing if Hampstead were to die in a duel with Thomas Earl.

"Ahhhh, Hampstead, you're a considerate man to remind us of rule number six. But if you'll recall, the crew, including yourself, put this to a vote and made Anne an equal. That being settled, let's discuss the matter at hand. If you feel that you cannot put this dispute behind you, it will be settled in a duel."

"Very well, Thomas Earl. … I challenge you to a duel."

Jack directs his attention to Earl. "Earl, what say you?"

"I accept Hempstead's challenge."

"Excellent. Gentlemen, the duel shall take place tomorrow on this spot at noon."

As Anne and Jack board the ship, Anne sees Mary, immediately walks to her and excitedly says, "Mary, there is to be a duel tomorrow between Robert Hempstead and Thomas Earl!"

Mary turns quickly toward Anne, "A duel with Thomas?"

"Yes, Earl and Hempstead."

Anne notices Mary's face fall slightly and enquires with a look.

Mary quietly confesses, "Thomas Earl and I have been together a number of times, and we have talked about the feelings we have for each other, and I will not allow a duel to take another man from me."

Anne suddenly remembers Mary's past and the loss of her husband to a duel, and says quietly, "Mary, I didn't know about you and Earl. We cannot allow this duel to take place. As Hempstead steps foot aboard our ship, we must cause a ruckus. Hempstead shall assault you, and I will be your witness."

"At least, you will act as if he did. No one will believe Hempstead over the two of us. You must make a loud fuss to attract the attention of the crew to you. Knowing that he has broken rule eight, you will challenge Hempstead to a duel on the spot. Trust me; the pig will not back down from a woman in front of the crew, fearing that he will look like a coward. I will get Jack to set the time of your duel before Thomas' duel with Hempstead. You will kill him during your duel."

Mary tells Anne, "If neither of us dies by pistol, we will continue the fight with cutlasses. The loser will be whoever bleeds first."

"You must provoke Hempstead into an action that would leave you no other choice but to end his life. Both of us know that Hempstead cannot strike the widest man by pistol. After he misses you, the duel will turn to cutlasses. You will then end his life. Thomas will not have an opportunity to duel."

Anne and Mary rush to the side of the ship where Hampstead is climbing aboard. Anne whispers, "As he grabs the length of rope to pull himself aboard, grab him, act as if you are struggling with him, and curse his name loudly." They lean over the side of the ship to see Hampstead reaching for the last length of rope. As he reaches, Mary leans forward, pulls his hand hard up against her chest, and begins violently to pull his arm back and forth to simulate that Hampstead is tearing at her shirt. Hampstead is totally caught off guard and has no clue what she is doing. He yells, "What in the bloody hell are you doing, Read?"

"You bastard, what did you just call me? Hempstead, you will regret hitting me!"

Hampstead is confused and yells in disbelief, "What? Damn it all, woman, let go of me ... let go of me, you bloody whore!"

While still holding Hampstead's arm, she throws a well-aimed punch that connects with Hampstead's eye, and then shoves his captive arm away from her. This motion causes his other hand to lose its grip on the rope, and he falls back into the longboat below. Mary quickly looks behind her to make sure that other shipmates have witnessed the scuffle, seeing a dozen or more of the ship's crew looking in her direction. She turns back to Hampstead and looks down to see him gathering himself after hitting the bottom of the longboat, and yells, "Hampstead, I challenge you to a duel."

"I accept your challenge, you crazy wench!"

Mary looks at Anne and delivers a slight smile, hearing the laughter of several shipmates.

Anne looks at the crowd watching and says, "Did you see that? Did you see Hempstead strike Mary?" One deckhand replies, "Aye Lass, I did!" Anne looks at Mary and whispers, "Love, we have our witness." She walks directly to tell Jack what has just happened and pleads with him to set the duel for the next morning at ten.

"Two duels for one man in one day is uncommon. Why is Mary in such a hurry to duel Hampstead, and why before Thomas Earl?"

"Hempstead has already fought with two mates in one day, Thomas Earl and Mary. He's like a rabid dog snapping at whatever comes near him. Why should he not fight two duels in one day? Earl will be out-skilled by Hampstead during their duel. You will lose a strong and reliable shipmate if he is killed. However, if you allow Mary to duel first, her superior skills with pistol and cutlass could rid you of Hampstead."

"My dear, your reasoning is sound. I will set the duel between Mary and Hampstead at ten tomorrow morn on the same shore that Hampstead will duel Earl two hours later."

Anne leaves Jack's cabin, finds Mary, and with a smile says quietly, "You will duel Hampstead tomorrow morn at ten."

The next morning the entire crew leaves the ship and assembles on the shore. At ten minutes before ten, the quartermaster allows Robert Hampstead to choose his pistol, and then Mary takes hers. The quartermaster informs them, "You shall stand with your backs together. On my count, you will take twenty paces in a straight line away from each other. At my command, you both will turn and fire. The duel will be over upon first blood. The person that draws first blood will be declared the victor. If no blood is drawn by pistol, the duel will then continue with cutlasses in the fighting style you choose. Again, upon the sight of first blood by cutlass, the duel will be finished, and the person that drew first blood will be declared the victor. Do you both understand what I have just told you?"

Mary and Hempstead both respond, "Yes."

At exactly ten o'clock, the quartermaster calls for Mary and Hampstead, telling them where to stand with their backs together. Thomas Earl fidgets nervously, holding his hat as he watches the two prepare. Anne makes sure to stand next to him during the duel telling him that all will be fine.

The opponents stand silently with their backs against each other. The quartermaster calls, "Ready? Begin your paces on my count—one, two, three. ... They continue their paces until they take their twentieth step. Thomas Earl anxiously grabs Anne's hand as the quartermaster yells, "Turn and fire!"

Mary and Hempstead turn simultaneously and take aim. Hempstead fires first. His shot zips only inches away from Mary's head. Mary stands motionless, still aiming her pistol toward Hempstead. She then purposely points her pistol toward the ground and pulls the trigger, shooting into the sand. The entire crew, including Hempstead, knows that he is no match fighting against Mary and her cutlass. Mary draws, smiles and begins walking toward Hempstead as he too draws his sword. Anne cannot stand the tension and yells, "Take him, Mary!" They swing, their swords crashing together violently. Hempstead fights hard and furiously. Each swing of his sword is much harder than it needs to be, as he hopes that his size and strength will take its toll on Mary and wear her down. Hempstead lunges forward in an attempt to run her through. Mary quickly sidesteps his blade, and, in one fluid motion, she moves from his side to his back, swings her cutlass hard in a downward motion and her cutlass's razor-sharp blade slices through the big man's Achilles tendon. He lets out a yell, tries to step up, and falls to his knees. Mary, still behind Hempstead, knows that she must finish him. She walks around his kneeling body to face him and says, "Hempstead, it appears I have drawn first blood, How does it feel having your foot chopped by a bloody whore?" To provoke him, Mary spits in his face and replaces her sword in its sheath. As she turns and begins to walk away, Hempstead grabs his sword and lunges at her back. She pulls her dagger, steps to the side and stabs Hempstead in his heart, killing him instantly. As she turns to walk away, she hears scattered compliments and several governed cheers from her shipmates. She looks toward Thomas, and he catches the slight smile on her lips.

Chapter Thirty-Four

A Good Careening

It is late October 1720. *The Vanity* is sailing off the coast of Jamaica, nearing Point Negril. In three weeks, Jack and his crew have taken one merchant ship and two fishing vessels. *The Vanity* is laden with the valuables taken from the raided ships. After sailing hard for months, it is in desperate need of repairs and a hull cleaning. The barnacles and other sea growth on the hull are beginning to take their toll, creating drag and slowing the ship's speed and maneuverability. If left on the hull for too long, it will eventually eat the wood away and separate the wooden planks, causing irreparable damage. Jack tells his quartermaster that this would be a good time to seek a secluded lagoon to careen the ship's underbelly.

Careening is a process that involves beaching the ship in shallow, sandy waters when the tide is high. At low tide, when the water level recedes, the hull of the ship is exposed.

The crew then uses towropes to pull the ship farther aground. After unloading most of the cargo, the men pull the ship onto each of side to make needed repairs while scraping the barnacles and other sea growth away from the hull.

Jack figures that the careening will take close to three days to complete. While the ship is being cleaned, he orders the crew ashore to forage for fruit and fresh water and to hunt game. When their work is done, Jack tells his crew that they will celebrate their recent victories with drinking, smoking, listening to music, and having friendly competitions of skill.

As they sail the Jamaican coast, they find the secluded lagoon they are looking for. The water leading into it is shallow for a good distance before meeting a sandy beach. Jack knows that these waters will prevent larger warships from getting too close to them, and the distance will keep them out of range of most cannons.

As the ship is beached and work begins, Anne and Jack take a walk along the shore. They shed their boots, opting for the comfort of the soft sand and cool ocean water. They begin to walk comfortably on the beach until *The Vanity* and crew disappear from sight. The late afternoon Jamaican sun intensifies and Jack stops and pulls his sweat-drenched shirt over his head to reveal his glistening body. Anne smiles, raises one eyebrow and says, "That's more like it, captain." They continue to walk only a few yards when Jack abruptly stops and begins to sit down. As he begins to fall backward onto the sand, he grabs Anne's hand and attempts to pull her down to join him. Anne suddenly pulls her hand away and laughs, "Jack, you might want to bask on this beach as a content seal would. I, however, would rather join the fish for a swim and cool my body. Jack smiles, "Love, you do just that. I will watch as you turn into a mermaid." Anne strips off her clothes in seconds and runs into the bellowing Caribbean surf. Jack watches as Anne playfully swims as the sun begins to set behind her. He lets out a sigh, stands and walks to the water's edge, strips naked and yells, "Will Amphitrite, the goddess of the sea, permit Poseidon to join her in the Jamaican sea?" Anne laughs as she pulls her water-soaked hair away from her face and answers, "Permission granted."

Jack grins and wades into the warm water, plotting a course to join Anne fifty feet from shore. As Jack draws closer to Anne, she smiles and extends her arm outward, beckoning him to take her hand. As they join hands, Jack pulls Anne against his body, "Annie, only months from now, our child will be born to this Earth. I realize that it will need a proper upbringing, one that will provide opportunity. Both you and I know that living a life among pirates will not provide this. I've spent much time reflecting on the life I've lived up to this point. Before meeting you, the only true love I've known has been captaining *The Vanity* and the freedom that it's given me. I realize that there is something I love more. What we have outweighs everything else. I will give up my ship and crew, without regrets, to be with you, raise our child and grow old together. With you to be always at my side, I have decided that I shall soon choose my replacement to captain *The Vanity*."

Anne lowers her head and begins to cry. Jack lifts her chin to kiss her mouth softly, then deeply, exploring the pleasures neither of them has felt nor given to another before.

CHAPTER THIRTY-FIVE

BARNETT'S MISSION

Three weeks earlier, Woodes Rogers summoned Captain Jonathan Barnett to his headquarters. Before leaving England for Nassau, Rogers hand-selected the people he needed to undertake the mission King George assigned to him. As the first governor of the Bahamas, he was to restore order to the Bahamas Islands and a good portion of the Caribbean Sea. His goal was to rid the region of all pirate operations, convert the pirates to privateers when possible, and have the privateers raise arms against England's enemies. Rogers has selected the people he knows he can count on to accomplish these goals. One of these individuals is Jonathan Barnett—a young, ambitious British naval officer who has made a name for himself by outthinking his adversaries and using aggressive tactics. The fact that Barnett has never lost a battle and is recognized as an innovative naval strategist impresses Rogers. He also knows that Barnett is a God-fearing man who can be trusted to be true to his word. He has a fondness for Barnett because, in many ways, he reminds Rogers of himself when he was a younger man.

After returning to New Providence from a routine patrol, Barnett receives word, via courier, that the governor would like to see him. He immediately leaves his ship and arrives at the governor's headquarters. As Barnett is shown into Rogers' office, the governor greets him. "Captain Barnett, I trust that you are keeping the flow of trade open for the Crown." Yes Governor, the trade routes are sound, and are indeed flowing. It's been months since I've had to board a single vessel."

"Very well. Let me get straight to the reason I have summoned you. I've received credible information that a ship meeting the description of *The Vanity* has been reported raiding merchant and fishing vessels off the coast of Jamaica. If you recall, it's been nearly eighteen months since we attempted to bring the captain of *The Vanity,* and a woman he keeps aboard his ship named Anne Bonny, into custody, only to find that they fled New Providence a day earlier. These two hold a special interest for me. I gave Governor Lawes my word that I would jail Anne Bonny for assaulting his sister-in-law at one of Chidley Bayard's galas, and this 'Calico Jack Rackham' chap has been a thorn in my side from the very moment I laid eyes on him. Rackham continues to practice piracy within my jurisdiction, and before fleeing New Providence, he shot one of my informants and took his wife. The woman I speak of just happens to be Anne Bonny.

"I need you to take three ships and sail the northwest coast of Jamaica. They were last reported there raiding a merchant ship near Lances Bay."

"Governor, with all due respect, if *The Vanity* sails off the coast of Jamaica, would this responsibility not lie with the governor of Jamaica and his fleet? Secondly, even though our intelligence tells us that this ship boasts larger guns than typical for a ship her size, I believe that raising three ships to overtake one sloop is more than what is needed. I can accomplish this with only one low draft sloop to manage the shallows, but if you insist that I employ more force, I will take one man-o'-war."

"Captain Barnett, I gave Governor Lawes my word that I would capture and jail Anne Bonny. She made me look foolish by escaping once, and I intend to keep my word. The fact that *The Vanity* is skirting the Jamaican coast has no bearing on what I promised the governor. If you are confident that you can manage with two ships, then so be it. Take your sloop and the man-o'-war *Albion*. Before dismissing you, I want to make myself perfectly clear. I do not want your confidence to cloud your judgment nor my expectations. Don't underestimate Rackham. He's proved to be a formidable adversary and has eluded capture before."

"Governor Rogers, rest assured I will complete this mission and deliver on your expectations. There is a reason why you selected me to head your fleet, and a reason why I've never lost a battle. You are correct that I have a great deal of confidence. I don't intend for Rackham and his ship to be my first defeat. When I locate the ship, how do you want me to handle the situation?"

"Sink *The Vanity* and its crew. No quarter is to be given. I would be elated if you were to capture Rackham, Bonny, and a few of his officers, delivering them to me alive. It's time that I make examples of them, as I have done with others, illustrating the fate of those choosing to remain on the account. If they die during your attack, all will not be lost. No trial or execution will save the Crown both time and money. Should that be the case, simply deliver the dead bodies of Rackham, Bonny, and a few of the crew to me."

CHAPTER THIRTY-SIX

TOO MUCH DRINK

After the crew's work is completed—the ship set upright, the cargo reloaded, and the ship anchored in the lagoon three hundred yards offshore—Jack, Anne, Mary and the crewmembers begin their victory celebration. They listen to music and dance about the deck. In their typical hard-drinking fashion, Jack and the crew drink until many of them either pass out or fall asleep where they sit on deck. Anne drinks, but not as much as Jack does. He eventually passes out below deck when fetching another bottle of rum. Mary is not the drinking type, but she dances with the best. Ajani does not drink; the intensity of hard liquor repulses him. He simply walks the deck amused by the crew's drunken behavior.

Everything begins to quiet down at nearly four in the morning. Anne and Mary sit next to each other, using the ship's side rail as a bench as their legs hang over the side. The two talk and laugh about their past experiences, facing a large full moon that is casting a bluish-white reflection across the lagoon and open water. Suddenly the mood turns serious and Anne confides, "Mary, there is something I need to tell. Now that I am with child, Jack and I plan to find a calmer life together. We will take our share of the ship's prize and settle in Cuba, raise this child and possibly have more." With mixed emotions, Mary stares out toward the water and replies, "Your decision does not surprise me. I reckoned the two of you would end up settling at some point." Mary then turns to Anne, smiles and says, "Anne, I am certain that I am with child, too, I think that the nights spent with Thomas Earl have lodged a seed."

The two women look at Thomas. He had passed out earlier and is seated close to them on top of a barrel. His body is propped up against the ship's mast, snoring loudly. As they continue to look at Thomas, his body flinches and briefly interrupts his snoring. Anne and Mary begin laughing uncontrollably.

Anne can barely form her words. "I left Jack in the same condition earlier."

"My God, Thomas sounds like a wounded warthog! He's a good man. Soon I reckon that we'll be faced with making the same decision that you and Jack have made."

After two days at sea, Barnett's ship locates the unsuspecting *Vanity*. Two lookouts spot the darkened silhouette of a ship anchored near the shore as they sail silently beyond the mouth of the lagoon. One of the watchmen uses his spyglass to get a better look. He sees the flickering flames and glowing of lanterns illuminating the deck. He is surprised to see a few motionless bodies of men sleeping on the deck.

"Be quick and notify Captain Barnett that, by all descriptions, we've found *The Vanity!* Report no activity on board, and it appears some of the crew are sleeping on her deck."

Anne suddenly stops in mid-conversation. "Mary, did you just hear something?"

"Are you referring to the flatulence coming from below deck?"

Anne stands up and scans the lagoon. "No, I thought I heard the sound of a ship's bell ringing in the distance."

"Anne … sit your arse back down and relax. You're hearing things." Mary laughs.

The watchman runs to Barnett's cabin and wakes him. The captain is informed that *The Vanity* is anchored in the lagoon they have just passed. He orders the watchman to wake the crew and man battle stations, and to do so in silence so as not to give away the element of surprise. Barnett knows that his slower-sailing man-o'-war, The *Albion,* has been ordered to trail his course by only a few miles. In the event they come across Barnett's sloop, they are to engage the enemy and position themselves on the far side of Barnett's ship to cut off *The Vanity's* access to the open ocean.

With only a few miles separating Barnett from the *Albion*, he estimates that he has less than a half hour to circle back around and launch a surprise attack against *The Vanity*. He calls to the quartermaster, "Have the helmsman turn our ship hard and about face, then with full speed sail into the lagoon to engage that ship. Have the master gunner, crew, and all cannons ready. As we approach, turn us quickly broadside and await my orders to open fire. I want us to be point blank when we release hell upon them."

Barnett's ship enters the mouth of the lagoon, sailing at full speed.

Anne and Mary are still talking when Anne sees Mary's smiling face instantly change to one of horror. Mary suddenly stops and jumps to her feet. "My God!"

Barnett's sloop turns hard to position itself broadside. Anne and Mary, in pure panic, begin yelling to their crew. Mary runs to the ship's bell, and as she passes Thomas, she pushes him. He falls from the barrel onto the deck but does not wake. Mary reaches the bell and rings it wildly.

Anne sees Ajani jump to his feet, already holding his cutlass in a confused state and turning his head from side-to-side, attempting to grasp the direction that their enemy is approaching.

Captain Barnett yells, "Fire lower guns!"

Mary sees the bright flashes of the enemy guns ignite. With no time to do anything else, she screams, "Hit the deck!"

Anne and Mary drop for cover. The ship is at such close

range that its cannon's grapeshot takes only a fraction of a second to reach them. All shots explode simultaneously against the side of the ship. The force of the explosions rocks them violently, rendering many of *The Vanity's* cannons facing Barnett's ship useless.

Five more shots explode on *The Vanity's* deck, sending shards of wood and molten metal ripping through the air. The shrapnel collides with the exposed men. Some are killed instantly. Several of the crew die where they had just recently been reveling. Anne raises her head slightly to see Ajani drop his cutlass, stagger, and fall overboard into the lagoon. Mary watches helplessly as a number of disoriented, bloodied men stumble about on the deck. One shipmate, in a confused haze, takes a step forward, only to fall flat with his leg blown completely off below his knee. She hears screaming and looks to see two others on fire, frantically jumping overboard in an attempt to save themselves.

A brief moment of silence falls, and then Barnett's quartermaster yells, "Fire!" The remaining British cannons are aimed higher to destroy *The Vanity's* mast and sails. The barrage pelts the ship, shredding the mainsail, tearing holes in the ship's headsail, and striking the side of the ship's heavy mast. As Anne remains facedown, she feels the concussion and heat radiating from the blasts. After the third salvo, she slowly raises her head again to assess the damage. As the smoke dissipates, she sees a large chunk missing from the mast. Severely weakened, the wood begins to creak. She hears two loud pops and the sounds of splintering wood and she knows that the mast is giving way. "Mary, mind the mast, it's falling!" she screams. Anne, Mary, and the few remaining survivors jump to their feet and quickly move clear of the mast as it buckles under the pressure of its own weight. The heavy wooden column collapses partially onto the deck and into the water away from Barnett's sloop. The surprise attack is devastating. In a matter of minutes, *The Vanity* is turned into a crippled smoldering hulk.

The women strain to see through the thick smoke billowing from the fires burning around them. The strong smells of gunpowder and the pungent odor of burning flesh are overwhelming. As some of the smoke clears, they see the deck strewn with the bodies of their shipmates.

Anne looks toward the attacking ship. The sight of the large, flowing British Union Jack glares in the light of the raging fires. Mary desperately calls out, "Anne, are you hit?"

"No. You?"

"I am not injured!" Barnett's sloop pulls close as Anne sees its crew hurling grappling hooks toward *The Vanity* and frantically yells, "They are boarding us! Where is everyone?" The two rush over to the hatch that leads below deck. They know that most of the crew retired there earlier after their heavy drinking. Anne looks into the ship's hold and sees a number of the men stumbling over each other, still in such a drunken state that they cannot function or comprehend the situation.

The British pull the ropes and the grappling hooks do

their job by digging into *The Vanity's* wooden deck. They quickly draw the two ships only feet apart and slam wooden planks down, creating bridges to board the ship.

Mary positions herself so that she and Anne are shoulder-to-shoulder, with their pistols and cutlasses drawn, growling, "Here they come!"

Anne yells at the drunken crew below deck, "Get your arses up here now!" The men are disoriented, and their lack of immediate response incenses Anne, unleashing her fury. She points her pistol and fires a shot below deck, striking one of the crew in his shoulder. She yells, "Jack, get them up here!" Anne pulls her other pistol from her belt and fires another round, hitting another crewmember in the face.

British troops swarm the ship's deck in a matter of seconds. The few men topside who try to fight are quickly cut down. The soldiers storm forward toward the two women. Mary drops her cutlass, pulls two pistols from her belt, and puts down two of them. She throws her guns at the approaching mass as she and Anne ready themselves to fight with their cutlasses.

Anne swings violently and chops at the neck of one while Mary swings her cutlass, making contact with two swords at once. Filled with adrenaline, they hear one of the troops yell, "These two are bloody women!" The British numbers are too great. Anne and Mary are wrestled to the ground, kicking and cursing their captors.

With the deck secured, Captain Barnett boards the ship.

He walks over to where his men are still struggling to contain Anne and Mary. He looks down at them and laughs quietly. "If you were men, you would have felt the blunt end of a musket's stock to calm you. I was told that there would be one hellcat aboard, not two." He then turns to his quartermaster, "Bring the women aboard with us. Treat them as you do the men." He walks to the hatch on the lower deck, where the remaining crew is trapped and being held at gunpoint.

He speaks in a loud and commanding voice. "If Captain Rackham is still alive below deck, I demand his immediate surrender along with any surviving officers of this ship. If you do not show yourself topside or I do not see Rackham's dead body before me, I will order my men to serve grenades to all below deck." All is silent, until the muffled sound of voices and footsteps are heard. Jack and his officers, still rum drunk, slowly climb the steps to the deck. Jack faces Barnett and says nothing. Barnett orders, "Take him and the others aboard. Put them in irons and lock them securely in the storage hold."

After the few prisoners are transferred to Barnett's sloop, the quartermaster asks, "Captain, what will you have us do with the others held below?"

"We are under orders to give no quarter other than to the prisoners that I was told to bring back. The governor has given me explicit orders to sink *The Vanity*. All those that survived our attack will sink with her. Secure that hatch."

"Aye, aye, captain."

Barnett orders the captain aboard *The Albion* to tow *The Vanity* to deeper waters outside the lagoon. They sink her, the remaining crew below deck drowning as he transports his prisoners to Port Royal.

Chapter Thirty-Seven

Pretrial Visit

Jack wakes on the morning of the trial to the sound of keys jangling and the voice of the jailer commanding him awake. As Jack rolls over to his side, he addresses the rude jailer, mumbling, "Now why in bloody hell would you be so cruel as to wake a man this early in the morn?"

Jack, now sitting on the side of his bed, rubs his face with both hands and yawns. He sees that the jailer has opened his cell door, and the large, clumsy-looking man stands in front of it, staring at Jack, motionless. Jack begins laughing at the man standing before him with an idiotic grin on his face, carrying a belly like that of a woman nine months pregnant. "So, mate, when are you due to release that baby you are carrying?" In response, the jailer's face turns from doorknob-dumb to that of an angry man. "Begging your pardon, sir Jack, I didn't mean to interrupt your slumber, but you have a visitor." The jailer grins from ear-to-ear as he moves to one side and reveals Woodes Rogers himself.

The sight of the governor standing at Jack's cell door catches Jack off guard. Jack's eyes become more intense as Rogers takes several slow steps forward, entering Jack's cell and looking him squarely in the eye. Jack recalls Rogers giving him the same cold stare a year earlier, when he and his crew passed him on their way out to sea as they left New Providence's harbor. Jack decides to break the silence first. "Governor Rogers, what brings you to converse with the likes of me? I would offer you a cup of tea, but it seems that the jailer will not afford me the luxury."

Rogers pauses, putting time between Jack's question and his reply. "Calico. Calico Jack. What an interesting name. I heard this name was derived from the brightly colored clothes you once wore as a free man. Seeing that they are not as bright to my eyes today, I don't really know how I should address you. I think I will call you by the Christian name that was given you at birth: "John." I believe that the Lord puts us on this earth with one of two paths to lead. One is a purposeful life, the path of good, serving the Lord, a life of advancing and contributing to humankind, being true to God, country and oneself, and the second being the path of evil. Some are born to serve the darker side unwittingly. Satan has a purpose for their lives, to cheat, steal, kill and destroy. You, your crew and the two hellcats that sailed aboard your ship are of course allies of the latter. John, I have to ask you, when you decided not to take the gracious pardon of his Majesty and chose to continue practicing piracy, did you really believe that I would forget about your public display of insubordination as you sailed your ship from New Providence? That night your face was etched into my mind. I vowed to myself if you ever returned to these waters, I would find you and your crew."

"Guv-nuh, as I suspected the moment we locked eyes, and as you have just confirmed, you are nothing less than a pompous peacock. You bloody puppets of the British Crown always seem to think that you are the masters of the world, and it's up to you to decide what you call your own."

Rogers interrupts and calmly says, "Pompous peacock? Rackham, you of all people calling someone else a pompous peacock! Look at yourself, how you dress in flamboyant and brightly colored clothing. If any man in this world should be called a peacock, it is you. However, you are correct about one thing. As a loyal subject of the British Crown and the governor of the Bahamas, I have the authority to take actions that I deem fit to advance the interests of King George. I came to you this morning to see if you might ask me for mercy. I see that this will not be the case. The trials for you and your men are simply formalities of our judicial system before finding you guilty of piracy. Yes, Rackham, I suspect that you and your men will be found guilty and swiftly put to death. I think that I will also allow the memory of your ways to live on after the hangman's noose has stretched your neck and you have soiled your pants. I will have your dead body tarred and feathered and placed in a cage on display, hanging from the point of the harbor to serve as a reminder to others of their fate should they choose to follow your ways."

Jack knows that with the jailer outside his cell and with Rogers being so close to him, he could easily make quick work of him by lunging for the governor's throat, grabbing and twisting it with both hands until it snaps. This would be the reaction that Rogers would expect of him, and Jack does not want to give him the satisfaction. He quickly tries to think of some sharp words that would infuriate Rogers, but cannot. He childishly sticks his tongue out and winks at him.

The only sound heard is a slight chuckle that comes from the thick jailer. Jack's unexpected response completely dumbfounds Rogers. He gives a confused look, turns and walks out of the cell without uttering a word. As the jailer slams the cell door, Rogers turns and says, "Oh, and, John, I forgot to mention that I was paid a visit by Sir Nicholas Lawes, the royal governor of Jamaica. It seems that Governor Lawes knows and has a special request for that whore you took aboard with you named Anne Bonny.

"It is said that some time ago she posed as a lady while attending one of Chidley Bayard's balls. Apparently, she saw fit to punch and knock out two of his sister-in-law's teeth. I thought that it might interest you to know that before Bonny is hanged, she will be publicly flogged, and all her teeth will be pulled from her head."

Jack looks at Rogers and sneers, "Guv-nuh, I will await your arrival in hell."

Chapter Thirty-Eight

The Trial

Anne and Mary are held in separate cells directly across from each other. Because they are women, their cells are located in a different building than those of the male crewmembers. They talk and believe that regardless of their gender, they also will be found guilty of piracy and sentenced to hang alongside their male shipmates. Anne knows that she is carrying Jack's child and shares an idea with Mary the day before the trial.

"Mary, Jack and the others will surely be found guilty of piracy and hanged. We, being women, will be an unusual aspect of the trial. I don't reckon that a woman has ever been subject to such. Our story and the reasons why we willingly practiced piracy with these men will become the focus of our trial. I was thinking of this and conjuring ideas that might cause the civilized members of the British court to think twice about hanging us alongside the rest of the crew."

"Other than us having cunnies and breasts—ah, I see the path you're headed down" … Mary trails off.

Anne says, "We will not be spared just because we are women, but I believe that the court will show us mercy since we are both with child. Our pregnancies are not far along, so our conditions will not be obvious to the court. We shall claim our bellies during the trial to play on their sympathies. Agreed?"

"Agreed."

Armed guards visit each of the cells where Jack and his crewmembers are kept. The guards place irons on the wrists and ankles of each man before leading them, in single file, to the large courtroom where their trial will take place. They are led into the courtroom, followed by the two guards leading Anne and Mary to their seats. All are wearing the same clothes as at the time of their capture. After living in dank jail cells for ten days without being allowed to bathe, their clothes are dirty, blood-spattered, and reeking of body odor.

Anne and Mary are placed in a row of chairs directly behind the eleven men. Anne sees Jack in the front row and thinks, *My God. He looks visibly older and tired. When he first introduced himself, he was so vibrant, confident and bold. Now he looks like a broken man.*

Jack looks around the courtroom and notices Anne looking at him. He flashes her a slight smile, and she looks away. Anne is still angered that they were taken captive because Jack and most of the crew ended up huddled below deck, too drunk to put up a fight as the British attacked their ship.

Everyone knows what the outcome of the trial will be before it begins. Rumors have been circulating for days that Governor Rogers has ordered all prisoners taken from *The Vanity* to be found guilty and swiftly executed, with no exceptions.

Since *The Vanity* was captured in Jamaican waters, the trial of the crew is held in Port Royal. Sir Nicholas Lawes, governor of Jamaica, presides over the vice admiralty court. As the trial begins, Lawes enters the courtroom wearing his black robe and customary long, white, curled wig. As he approaches the bench, all are asked to rise. He is announced to the court and takes his seat. All in the courtroom are told to be seated.

Lawes reads the charges. "The prisoners are charged as follows: the captain of the pirate ship *Vanity* is John Rackham, alias Calico Jack. The crew of the same ship is George Featherston, Thomas Bourn, Thomas Earl, John Howell, Patrick Carty, John Davies, James Dobbins, Richard Corner, Noah Harwood and John Fenwick. The four charges against the prisoners are as follows:

"1. That they did practically, feloniously, and in a hostile manner attack, engage, and take seven certain fishing boats. They assaulted the fishermen, stole their fishing boats, their fish, their fishing tackle, and marooned all surviving crew.

"2. That they did upon the high seas, in a certain place, at a distance of about three leagues from the island of Hispaniola, set upon, shoot at, and take two certain merchant sloops, and did assault, murder, and maroon this vessel's captain and crew.

"3. That on the high sea about five leagues from Port Maria Bay on the island of Jamaica they did fire upon and take a schooner, murdered its captain, most of the ship's crew, put other mariners in corporeal fear of their lives and did assault, murder, and maroon this vessel's crew.

"4. That about one league from Dry Harbor Bay, Jamaica, they did board and enter a merchant sloop called *Mary*, did steal and carry the sloop and her tackle away, and did assault, murder, and maroon this vessel's captain and crew.

The trial lasts for only three days. Captain Barnett, along with several seamen and fishermen who managed to survive being marooned, give their testimony. Jack and his men are found guilty and sentenced to be hanged by the neck until dead.

Because Anne and Mary are women, they are tried separately from the men. After the focus of the trial shifts to Anne and Mary and all testimony is heard, Governor Lawes prepares to render his verdict. Lawes routinely asks Anne and Mary, "As to any of the condemned, do you have anything further to say?" Anne speaks for both herself and Mary. "Yes, Guv-nuh, we do. Both Mary Read and I plead our bellies." The courtroom is astounded by Anne's unexpected announcement.

Governor Lawes sinks in his chair, quickly gathers his thoughts and calls for order in the courtroom. By law, the court cannot take the life of an unborn child by executing the mother. Lawes addresses Anne and Mary. "The fact that the two of you are harboring innocence in your bellies will not change the crimes you have committed, nor shall it prevent this court from carrying out its judgment and your punishment. You, Mary Read, and you, Anne Bonny, are to go from here back to your cells to await the birth of your children. After which, you shall both be hanged by the neck 'til dead. May God, in his infinite goodness, be merciful to both your souls."

The sentenced men are marched out of the courtroom. As they are led from the room, Anne and Jack briefly look into each other's eyes. As the two women are led from the room, they hear the whispers of the onlookers in the crowded gallery. Anne feels hundreds of people watching her as she and Mary pass. She hears a woman's voice pointedly yell, "Whores!" Anne quickly turns her head to catch sight of the woman who dared call out. She glances into the crowd and sees a familiar face watching her from the mass of spectators. Chidley Bayard has come to the court to see Anne for the last time. His eyes follow her as she is swiftly led out.

Chapter Thirty-Nine

Last Request

The day before Jack and his crew are hanged, he is granted a last request. He asks to be granted a final conversation with Anne. She is brought to his cell, where they are given permission to spend ten minutes together. As the cell door is closed behind her, the two momentarily stare at each other without saying a word. Jack breaks the silence. "Even after living in a cell all this time, you are still the most beautiful creature I've ever known. Annie, since being confined to this prison, I realize that my decision to continue pirating, instead of taking the pardon Rogers served up, has condemned us all. Tomorrow, before the noose snaps my neck, I will ask God to forgive us for our sins and watch over our child after we are gone."

As their time runs out, the jailer tells Anne, "Lass, it is almost time." Anne looks into Jack's eyes and says, "I will never forget our time together, the riches we sought, the passion we shared, but to this day my biggest regret is not knowing what would have happened if you and the crew had fought Mary and I that night we were captured."

Jack replies, "Annie, that's something no one will ever know. One thing I am certain of is that even as this life ends, my love for you will not die. I will look up from hell to search the heavens for you, knowing that our spirits will live on through our child."

Anne takes Jack's hands, her eyes filling with tears as she attempts to hold back her emotions. "I will miss you, Jack, but in all finality, I cannot forgive you."

"Annie, it was a shame that I, and most of our men, were caught in such a pickled state. I could not walk, let alone see straight. I would have swung my cutlass at Barnett's twin as his duplicate cut me down. Think what you will, but know if I had only half my wits about me, I would have been on the deck fighting at your side. At the moment of the Brits' barrage, I recalled Bartholomew's account of the battle fought between Teach and Maynard.

Maynard ordered his crew to remain below deck, undercover, until the firing stopped. I found myself in a similar predicament and thought it wise to borrow Maynard's strategy. I ordered the crew to remain below deck until the explosions ceased. Within seconds after their cannons stopped, the Brits were on top of us firing at us from above and down into the hold. We were trapped, under siege. Left with no other options, I surrendered *The Vanity* to Barnett."

After hearing Jack's account of what he believed transpired during the battle, Anne realizes for the first time that he does not know that she was the one firing into the ship's hold. She immediately dismisses the notion that she could be the reason why Jack chose not to fight and to surrender his ship and crew; that he and the crew chose to hide and not fight because they simply were too drunk. Anne replies, "Jack, you can choose to justify your actions as you see fit, but consider this, if you and the others had fought the Brits like men, we need not be hanged like dogs."

The jailer tells Anne, "Lass, it is time for you to go." Anne looks at Jack and says, "I will miss you. As she walks from the cell, she turns and says, "Do not give the Brits the satisfaction of seeing fear in your eyes when you are led to the gallows."

Two days after being sentenced, Jack, George Featherston, Richard Corner, John Davis, and John Howell are transported from their prison cells to Port Royal at Gallows Point. The other condemned men are transported to Kingston where they will be executed the following day.

Early in the morning of the eighteenth day of November 1720, Jack and the others are taken from their cells and marched outside by four armed guards to the prison's courtyard. Jack says, "Look mates, the guv-nah was kind enough to send us a special carriage to deliver us to our destiny." The lead guard turns his head sharply and shouts, "Rackham, keep your mouth shut!" Before entering the reinforced prison wagon, Jack hears the cry of a seagull above him. He looks skyward to see a lone gull riding an updraft of wind. The white bird instinctively maneuvers its body to create the lift needed to maintain its nearly stationary position. The bird lets out another cry, dips one wing, and effortlessly glides down to the courtyard's ground, landing some distance away from the wagon. A guard passes, paying no attention to the bird, as he nearly kicks it with his polished black boots. The gull squawks, takes a few deliberate hops, and flies away. Jack follows the bird as it disappears over the prison wall. With the gull now out of sight, his attention is shifted to the blue cloudless sky. He thinks to himself ... *the sky seems bluer today ... more brilliant*. His daydream is soon interrupted when he feels the butt of the guard's musket connecting to the middle of his back, shoving his body forward, and hears, "In you go, Rackham."

They travel only a short distance before stopping the wagon. The silence within the wagon is broken by the clanking sounds of the guard's key being placed into the large, iron padlock that holds Jack and his men captive. The back doors of the wagon fly open, causing them to squint their eyes, giving them a moment to adjust fully to the bright sunlight. The guard commands, "Everyone out and no talking." They all climb out of the wagon and see the imposing wooden structure before them that was constructed for only one purpose. With their hands and legs restrained by shackles, Davis and Howell are the first to be led up the wooden staircase to the platform, followed by Featherston, Corner, and finally Jack. They can thank a thousand-year-old custom that the British adopted from the Roman army, which occupied Great Britain for hundreds of years. The custom always has the lowest ranking officers executed first so that their commander can watch them die before him.

Davis and Howell are hanged first. Then the guard leads Featherston to stand on the center of the platform where the noose is positioned directly above him. Jack and Corner stand behind him. As the guard nudges him forward three steps and back a half, he tells him, "Stand here and do not move."

Jack looks over at the minister standing at the corner of the platform. He looks the minister up and down and rests his gaze on the weathered-looking hands clutching a worn Holy Bible. The minister looks at Jack and they lock eyes. The minister immediately shifts his eyes back toward Featherston. Jack thinks, *What an odd predicament we are all in now.* As Jack and his men stand behind Featherston, they see him look up toward the hangman's noose, then down to his feet where a large red "X" is painted in the center of a square hatch. Jack hopes that their executioner is experienced at his craft. He has personally witnessed five hangings in his life. Three went as planned, and the other two were botched. These two were etched permanently into his mind. The noose has to be fitted just right in order for a hanging to be successful. If it is too loose, an individual dies a hard death by strangulation. The body will jerk and kick when dying and twitch uncontrollably even after death. The victims of botched hangings eyes often protrude from their sockets and their tongues swell to five times their normal size. On the other hand, if the noose is too tight, an individual's head can be pulled right off its body.

If the hangman has done his job correctly, the hatch will fly open, sending Featherston's 165-pound body into a brief free-fall that will abruptly stop as the length of rope reaches its end. The rope and gravity will work together to end his life. Featherston's own body weight will snap his neck at the base of his skull. His fractured vertebra will push into his brain stem, creating what is called a "hangman's fracture."

Jack sees Featherston begin to tremble and fears that he is about to break down. Jack tries to calm his friend, "George, don't think about what is to happen. Think about one moment in your life that pleased you most." Without moving his body, Featherston turns his head back toward Corner and Jack and gives them a tentative half-smile. The minister takes two steps forward and begins reading a passage from the Bible. Featherston turns his head to look forward as the noose is tightened around his neck. The wooden lever is pulled, the hatch flies open, and George falls and disappears from sight. The rope springs and is pulls taut.

The guard walks over, grabs Corner by his arm, and leads him to stand in front of the hatch. Two men below work quickly to remove Featherston's dead body from the grip of the noose. All is made ready for Corner. The hatch is reset.

As the noose is fitted, Corner says, "Jack, I'm thinking about the time when we could not find wind. We were stranded, left baking in the hot sun. The entire crew believed we were doomed. I remember the incredible feeling of happiness that came over us when we saw the wind finally catch our sails." Corner releases a big smile. He hears the minister finish reading his passage and says, "Goodbye, Jack." The hatch lever is pulled and he too, is hanged.

Minutes later, Jack is moved to stand on top of the hatch. He says nothing, as he is the last to go. As the executioner fits the noose around his neck, Jack whispers, "Lad, if you would be so kind as to do your best work." Jack then closes his eyes and takes a deep breath. The first thought that enters his mind is himself as a seven-year-old boy looking over the green English countryside. A brisk breeze envelops him. He looks up to see his father standing at his side. They hold hands as they walk together through the tall grass toward an enormous stone wall. Jack remembers being confused about why such a towering wall would have been built in the middle of nowhere, seemingly without reason or purpose. His father picks him up, sets him onto his broad shoulders, and walks up a stout hill to stand next to the stone wall. Young Jack inquires, "Father, how did it get here?"

Jack's father responds, "John, a great king named Hadrian, who ruled over a vast empire, ordered his army to build this wall across our entire country to protect us from our enemies to the north." Jack looks at the wall as far as he can see.

His thoughts then shift to himself as a young man, taking his first voyage as a deckhand aboard a British merchant ship. As the ship leaves the harbor, Jack breathes in the salty air and looks up to the burgeoning sails. The bright sun blinds his eyes.

His thoughts then shift to Anne, seeing her smile as he

takes her hand for the first time at a small table inside the Goat's Head Tavern. He remembers making love to her for the first time in their bed aboard *The Vanity*. Jack's thoughts are broken as he begins to hear the minister reading a Bible verse only a few feet from his ear. Jack opens his eyes and glares at him. "With all due respect, Father, I don't need your hollow words cast upon me. Save them for someone that truly needs them, as I know my destination." The minister obliges, stops reading, and uncomfortably clears his throat. He takes several steps backward to his corner on the platform. Jack closes his eyes and recaptures his interrupted thought. Anne is lying by his side as they stare into each other's eyes for what seems to be an eternity. She smiles at him. The hangman pulls the lever. Jack feels the sudden movement of the hatch flying open under his feet and quickly takes in his last breath.

The five bodies are stacked on top of each other and unceremoniously carted off into the stone building adjacent to the gallows. A jailer lifts the bodies of Jack, Corner, and Featherston from the cart and places them on a large wooden table. The jailer leaves the room and returns carrying two large buckets. The man draws a large brush from one of the buckets and spends an hour painting three thinly layered coats of tar onto their clothing and skin. The next morning the tarred bodies are taken down and hanged in gibbets, one at Plumb Point, one at Bush Key, and the other at Gun Key. Davis and Howell's bodies, along with the others executed in Kingston, are taken to a local graveyard and buried in unmarked graves.

CHAPTER FORTY

AN AGREEMENT STRUCK

Anne's incarceration begins to weigh heavily on James. No matter what he does, his thoughts turn to Anne in her small, cold stone cell. Even though Anne left him and is carrying Rackham's child, he cannot deny the deep feelings he still has for her. Knowing that the court has passed judgment condemning her to be hanged after the birth of her child, James cannot bear the thought of Anne meeting her end on the gallows by the hangman's noose as Rackham and his crew had months earlier. He knows that the only hope of saving her is to sail back to Charles Towne and plead with her father somehow to influence Governor Rogers to pardon Anne and release her from prison.

News of the capture, judgment, and demise of Rackham and his crew has recently arrived in Charles Towne. Upon hearing the news, William Cormac thinks, as others do, that justice has been served and the world is a better place with fewer pirates. Since disinheriting Anne after her marriage to James, Cormac has had no clue as to what has become of them or that Anne is among the rogues who have been captured, tried, and condemned.

The evening that James arrives in Charles Towne, he leaves the ship and travels directly to Cormac's estate. He is not warmly received. However, the fact that Anne is not accompanying James earns him an audience. Hat in hand, James is led into Cormac's parlor, where he explains the events that have led him back to Charles Towne.

Cormac is compelled to save his daughter, but with conditions. He realizes that he has the upper hand on James. He despises him and will not forgive him for marrying his daughter. "If I am to find a way to secure Anne's release from prison, you, sir, must agree that your marriage to Anne will be annulled through the church, and you will never again set foot in Charles Towne or contact Anne or her child."

James has no choice but to agree to Cormac's terms. He stands and walks toward the large window in Cormac's parlor. "Agreed," he says, and continues, "Sir Cormac, I must tell you that I have had business dealings with Guv-nuh Rogers. He is a ruthless man. He does not give in lightly. For us to free Anne from the court's sentence and have the Guv-nuh of Jamaica pardon her, we will need the backing of someone who has a great deal of influence and power."

"Who in the Caribbean has that kind of influence?"

"A man named Chidley Bayard."

"Tell me what you know of Bayard and the influence you say he has."

"Chidley Bayard is considered the wealthiest man in the Caribbean. My dealings at Guv-nah Rogers' office allowed me to overhear many conversations. I heard the Guv-nah speak several times about how Bayard's merchant trading fleet generates a tremendous amount of wealth for the Crown through taxation of the goods he imports. It's also a common belief that, in addition to taxation, Bayard pays Rogers and other officials undocumented fees in order for his ships to dominate trade in the region's ports.

"And there is something else that I must tell you. After sailing to New Providence, the stress of not being able to find gainful employment began taking its toll on my marriage to your daughter. I am ashamed and truly embarrassed to inform you that during this time, I drank heavily and had relations outside our marriage with numerous women. Anne discovered my adultery and took my actions to heart. I tell you this, not as a confession to seek absolution, but to explain to you that I believe my actions created the circumstances for Anne to have a relationship with Bayard before sailing with Rackham and his crew. You might view Anne's adultery as a flaw in her character, but I realize now that I was the weaker one and am the one to blame."

As Cormac listens to James confessing his sins, he gives him a blank stare to conceal the deep-seated emotions that suddenly flood his mind. In a matter of seconds, he silently relives the many times that he gave in to his weakness for women and Irish whiskey. His betrayal broke his wife's heart, and his disregard for her feelings hurt her even more. His selfish actions collapsed their marriage. To thwart his feelings, he stands from his desk and walks a short distance to his parlor window. As he looks out, he continues to revisit his past. James' voice quickly becomes muffled background noise. Looking back, Cormac does not blame Rachel for making sure that all in County Cork knew of his adultery to ruin his reputation purposely.

Leaving his wife and his country behind for Mary Brenan and Anne provided him with the anonymity needed to build a new life. No one in America knew about his past or the fact that Anne was born an illegitimate child. Even though he is a self-centered man, all the years that have passed have not dissipated his guilt. Cormac realizes the pain that he caused his former wife. His guilt is like a persistent wound that never fully heals but remains open and festering. Cormac goes for months without thinking of his past, but when he does, he sometimes spirals into a deep depression, drinking heavily for days.

As Cormac regains his focus, he tells James, "Lad, most believe that good and evil are polar opposites. I, on the other hand, believe that good and evil are close neighbors, with very little distance separating the two. Circumstances, decisions, good fortune and bad can turn a sinful man to a life of virtue or a virtuous man to a life of selfish decadence."

Cormac suddenly realizes that his self-indulgent soul

searching could be making him appear weak. He quickly looks James in the eye and says, "Knowing what I just told you, don't think for a second that my beliefs in the human spirit put us any closer than we were before I learned of your existence."

Not knowing Cormac's past, James does not understand the reference, but out of respect for the man, he replies, "Indeed, Sir Cormac."

James pauses and regains his thoughts. "I traveled here to see you because I believe that Bayard is the only person who carries the influence needed to gain Anne's release, but knowing how their relationship ended, I am not sure if he will entertain the thought. There could only be two reasons why Bayard would even consider meeting with me and approaching the governor for Anne's release. First, if he has any remaining feelings for Anne and second, if he could use our situation for his own financial gain.

After a moment, Cormac responds, "I will make arrangements for us to sail to the Bahamas Islands immediately. Before you leave, provide my house servant with the name of the inn where you are staying. I will send word of our departure to you in advance."

"Very well, sir, and thank you." As James leaves Cormac in his parlor, Cormac says, "Oh, and James, speak nothing of our conversations to anyone; this is our business and our business only."

James nods his head as he leaves the room.

Cormac charters the first available ship to sail to New Providence. During the voyage, James becomes Cormac's shadow. James' nervous energy becomes an annoyance to him. He begins to stay clear of James and avoids him at every turn. He does not want such simple-minded small talk to interfere and cloud his thoughts while considering possible angles he can explore with Bayard. Cormac's first decision is that he will not portray himself as the desperate father, traveling to New Providence to beg for Bayard's help to gain his daughter's freedom. Instead, he will present himself as a businessman exploring ways that Anne's release could be used, in conjunction with other options, to benefit Bayard financially.

Cormac knows one fact before even meeting with Bayard. If he is the richest man in the Caribbean, then he's an astute entrepreneur. A man who achieves this much wealth and power typically conspires ways to achieve more. If Cormac can help identify approaches to leverage Bayard's business dealings with Woodes Rogers, Nicholas Lawes, and the British Crown for greater gain, Bayard may consider using his influence to gain Anne's freedom as payment.

Cormac tells James, "You must know that the extent of your role in this negotiation will simply be to guide me through the unfamiliar surroundings of New Providence and supply me with information if I need it. Under no circumstances are you to attempt to make contact with Chidley Bayard or Governor Rogers unless I ask you to. If I do call upon you for this reason, I will be extremely clear as to what I want from you. Understood?"

Cormac has never been to New Providence and does not know the dynamics of the land and its people. If he needs to locate specific people or resources, having James available will serve a purpose. Cormac gives James a modest amount of money and tells him, "This money is to keep you busy while we are in New Providence. This payment is intended to fill your idle time. That being said, I trust that you will not go astray. Stay close, but don't come looking for me. If I need you, I will find you. Now where will I find Bayard?"

James replies, "As our ship entered port, I recognized three of Bayard's ships at the docks. I reckon he is in New Providence, I am sure that he will be at his estate."

"Very well. I will send a courier tomorrow morning requesting an audience with him."

That evening, Cormac drafts a brief letter to Bayard.

Esteemed Mister Bayard,

It would do me a great honor if I could meet with you this afternoon at your estate, or a time and place of your choosing. It would be my privilege to introduce myself and to converse with you regarding a matter of utmost importance.

With sincerity and respect, I am your faithful and obliging servant,

William Cormac

Charles Towne, Carolina

Cormac sends his letter to Bayard early the next morning

and promptly receives a response from Bayard.

Mister Cormac,

Although I would enjoy having the opportunity to meet with you, my current business affairs will not permit such, on such short notice. If your future travels bring you to New Providence again, please send me a letter in advance with a brief explanation regarding the matters in which you would like to discuss. Given advanced notice, I would be more than happy to schedule a meeting with you.

I am, sir, your most humble and obedient servant,

Chidley Bayard

Cormac reads the letter from Bayard and in a quiet voice simply says, "Unacceptable."

Bayard's rejection was unexpected. As a prominent member of colonial society in Charles Towne, Cormac has grown accustomed to commanding attention. He is not used to rejection, and he does not like anyone showing disrespect for the position he has fought so hard to gain. Cormac's ego clouds the reality of the fact that his social position in Charles Towne means nothing in New Providence. Although, he does understand that being a stranger to Bayard and requesting an impromptu meeting with him could be seen not only as an inconvenience, but also as an annoyance. Still, Cormac finds Bayard's response unacceptable and decides to summon a carriage to take him to the man's estate.

Cormac arrives at the Bayard Estate early that afternoon. One of Bayard's house servants cordially asks his name and if

Sir Bayard is expecting his visit. Cormac responds by saying, "Please inform Mister Bayard that I have traveled far to gain an audience with him, and that I would appreciate it if he could spare a brief moment from his busy schedule to speak with me." The servant responds, "Very well, Mister Cormac. I will inform Sir Bayard of your request." Minutes later, the servant returns and informs Cormac, "I am sorry Mister Cormac, but Sir Bayard is indisposed and cannot meet with you. He asked if you could be so kind as to schedule a meeting with him on a later date."

"Please inform Sir Bayard that William Cormac is the father of Anne Bonny and that I have traveled from Charles Towne, Carolina to speak to him today."

"I shall do so." The servant turns and walks with a faster pace down the hall to deliver the new message. He returns more quickly this time, "Mister Cormac, please follow me. Sir Bayard will meet with you in his study."

Halfway down the long, opulently decorated hall, the servant turns to open the two large doors of Bayard's study. As they walk into the room, the servant announces, "Sir Bayard, Mister William Cormac" and departs, closing the doors behind him. Cormac looks at the man seated behind a large wooden desk cluttered with piles of business documents. Bayard continues to sign several of them and does not acknowledge Cormac's presence. Without making eye contact, Bayard says, "Mister Cormac, please be seated and make yourself comfortable. I will be with you in a moment." After a moment, Bayard places his quill pen aside.

"Sir, I did not understand your persistence and urgency to have a conversation with me until my servant informed me that you are the father of Anne Bonny. With this news, I understand. However, I am confused about why you would want to meet with me rather than meeting with Governor Rogers or Governor Lawes of Jamaica."

"Mister Bayard, thank you for taking time out of your busy schedule to meet with me. I was informed that my daughter, Anne, has been tried and convicted of piracy, having sailed aboard a ship named *The Vanity*. In meeting with you, I hope to explore avenues that I can take to convince Governor Lawes to grant her a pardon. I would like to have her released to my custody in order to take her home to Charles Towne. I understand that you have a great deal of influence with your business dealings in this region and that your merchant fleet provides the British Commonwealth with important trade and imported goods that are essential for the successful growth of the Caribbean Islands. This being said, I was hoping that you could use your influence for leverage in convincing the governor to gain Anne's release from her pending sentence."

"Well, Mister Cormac, I now find myself in an even more confused state regarding the meaning of your visit. The British Crown and I don't always agree on certain things, such as the high degree of taxation placed on the goods I continue to import to these islands. We have found ourselves at odds on many occasions. However, on the subject of piracy, we do agree that it must be vanquished. I have had three ships, in as many years, raided and relieved of their cargos. When Governor Rogers landed in New Providence, he extended the offer of a full pardon to those practicing piracy in this region. He made it clear to all that if they continued to practice piracy, they would be caught and tried for breaking the king's laws. You see, it is important to both my merchant fleet and the British government to maintain order in these waters. If your daughter made the decision to practice piracy, then I cannot see why the fate and consequences of her decision should be my concern."

Suddenly, William Cormac's background as a trial lawyer in Ireland takes over. It is Cormac's nature to take the opposing view, to cross-examine. He instinctively feels, by observing the sudden shift in Bayard's body language and change in his tone of voice, that Bayard is attempting to cover a weakness. Cormac stands from his chair and begins walking at a slow pace around Bayard's study, a technique learned to project a position of authority and to make the person on the stand more anxious and more apt to confess guilt. Cormac knows that he must control himself. He does not want to go too far with the game he's playing. He needs Bayard as his ally, not his enemy.

"Mister Bayard, I feel that I must talk frankly. I assume that since learning that I am Anne's father and that Anne's name is not mine, you would understand my intention of wanting to meet with you. Before leaving Charles Towne, I learned that it is common knowledge that you and Anne became very close to each other and she stayed at your estate as your houseguest. I will not judge the relationship you two had or the fact that my daughter was your mistress, but ..."

Bayard quickly interrupts, "Mister Cormac, With all due respect, I cannot see how the relationship between two consenting adults could be at issue, or is any of your concern." "Agreed, but only if the two adults consenting were not tied to holy matrimony. Mister Bayard, Anne was married while she slept with you in your estate. She is still legally married to her husband, James Bonny. Did you not also know that Anne has been carrying a child now for nearly eight months? That term, compared with the day you asked her to leave your estate, could be terribly suspect for those who enjoy consuming this type of information."

Bayard responds in a raised and agitated voice, "Mister Cormac, you requested to have a conversation with me in my home. Being a gracious man, I allowed it. Now you make accusations that are coming close to sounding as if you could be threatening blackmail. I will not allow you to speak to me in this manner nor will I continue to entertain this conversation. I believe that this meeting is finished!"

"Mister Bayard, it is not my intent to slander your good name or the reputation that you have worked so hard to achieve, nor are my sights on blackmail. I only point out that I am here, in New Providence, to take any means necessary in saving the life of my daughter. You cannot be certain that the child she carries is not yours. Do you want to live with the fact that you had it within your power to save Anne's life and the life of her child, but chose otherwise? I think not. This would be too heavy a burden to carry for the rest of your life."

Bayard responds now in a calmer voice, "Mister Cormac, I believe that you have said all you intended to say. I have nothing further to add to this conversation. I will weigh my decision whether or not to meet with Governors Rogers and Lawes. If you do not hear from me within two days, then all will remain on its present course. I bid you good day."

Cormac returns to New Providence and the inn where he is staying, and begins to wonder if he made the right decisions during his conversation with Bayard. He firmly believes that if he had not played the cards he held, Bayard would not even be considering the idea of using his influence to gain Anne's freedom. As time passes, he begins to grow nervous. He does not receive word from Bayard after the first day or evening, and he wonders whether Bayard is playing a cruel game with him. Cormac fears that Bayard will not consent to help Anne and will attempt to force his hand to see if he pursues blackmail.

The next morning, Cormac looks from his window to see a courier stop and tie his horse to the post outside the inn. He quickly walks to the entrance as the courier delivers the envelope addressed to him. The innkeeper takes the envelope and calls out, "Sir Cormac, a message has arrived for you."

Cormac quickly breaks the wax seal and opens the envelope. He unfolds and reads a letter that consists of only three sentences.

Mister Cormac,

I have made the decision to meet with Governors Rogers and Lawes for reasons I will keep to myself. I suggest that you remain in New Providence for the remainder of this month. I will send word to you soon.

With sincerity and respect,

Chidley Bayard.

CHAPTER FORTY-ONE

THE DEAL

Two days have passed since the conversation took place between Cormac and Bayard. Chidley Bayard decides to pay an unannounced visit at the governor's office. The governor's assistant enters Rogers' office to inform him that Chidley Bayard has requested a brief conversation with him. Rogers responds, "Of course, show Sir Bayard to my office. I always have time for him." As Rogers finishes his sentence, Bayard enters the room. "Governor, thank you for taking the time to meet with me. I understand how taking meetings from unannounced visitors can be bothersome. Just the other day, I had a complete stranger insist on meeting with me."

"A complete stranger? How bloody annoying."

"Indeed, it was ..." Bayard continues, "Governor Rogers, I wanted to pay you a visit this morning to commend you and your office on ridding our waters of the raider scourge. I've not had one ship raided or one report of piratical activities in nearly a year. The last news I have heard about pirates in these waters involved your sending Captain Barnett to capture Jack Rackham's crew and their ship *The Vanity*. I understand that Rackham and the surviving members of his crew were tried, found guilty and hung. What became of the two women found sailing aboard the ship? "

"Well ... as I am sure you know, the two females pled their bellies and were granted a stay of execution until they birth their children. I received word that one of the females died of fever in prison and will not attend her meeting atop the gallows with the hangman's noose."

Bayard is caught off guard with this news and has a hard time concealing his emotions. "Which of the two perished?"

"Ah, yes, forgive me Sir Bayard. I nearly forgot that you had a relationship with Anne Bonny before she left New Providence to sail with Rackham and his crew."

Bayard understands that Rogers already knew that Anne was his mistress and of all that took place the night he asked her to leave his estate. Bayard senses that Rogers is toying with him and not telling him the name of the dead female for his own twisted amusement.

"Yes, Governor Rogers, I think we are both well aware of my past relationship with Anne Bonny. Now, again, which female perished?"

"Oh, yes, sorry, how very rude of me ... Mary Read."

"Well Governor, that is a bit of good news. I would hate

to have wasted your time today by coming here to ask you to convince Governor Lawes to pardon a woman that is now dead."

"I beg your pardon?"

"No, my good governor, no need to beg my pardon. I only need a pardon for Anne Bonny."

"What are you speaking of? I don't understand?"

"What do you not understand? As a personal favor, I will need you to convince Lawes to pardon Anne Bonny."

"Mister Bayard, are you resurrecting misguided feelings that you have for a past lover? As I recall, after Bonny so gracefully knocked two teeth from the governor's daughter-in-law's head, you judiciously removed her from your home. I made a vow to Governor Lawes that I would locate her, see to her capture, and deliver her to him for justice."

"Governor Rogers, you are not in a position to question what I ask of you. Need I remind you that I hold the power to control commerce in this region? My reasons are my own and no one else's."

"Mister Bayard, I cannot pardon Anne Bonny. She has already been convicted of piracy, and as soon as she gives birth to her unborn child, her death sentence will be carried out. Governor Lawes himself passed down her sentence."

"Governor, I don't think you understand, I am not asking you to grant Anne Bonny a pardon, I am telling you to grant her a pardon."

"Mister Bayard, everyone knows that you are a very influential man in this region. However, you cannot order me to do anything. I represent the king, and what I decide as the Governor of the Bahamas is sovereign law."

"Yes, you are technically correct, but please indulge me. I cannot order you, but I can illustrate why it would be in the best interest of you and Governor Lawes to grant Anne Bonny a pardon. If you do as I ask, your reward will be that all will remain the same. Nothing will change, and business will take place as it has. If you do not do as I ask, then I am prepared to leave New Providence. I will move my merchant fleet operations and all my business dealings to a Colonial American port, such as Boston, Philadelphia or even Charles Towne. I am sure that the other British officials there will enjoy the large amounts of money generated through their docks from the taxation of my imported goods. I am also convinced that the special consideration fees that I pay personally to you and Lawes would be greatly missed by you both. If you want to continue to receive this allowance, then you will do as I say with no questions asked."

"Well Mister Bayard, the hand you just dealt commands attention. I will discuss this matter with Governor Lawes and inform him of your proposition and the reasons why he must grant Anne Bonny a pardon. I am sure that he will agree that trading her, to keep you and your fleet in place, is a small price to pay."

"This is how I would like Bonny's pardon to be projected to both citizens and to your superiors ... Anne Bonny, tried and convicted of piracy, was sentenced to die by hanging. Since her conviction, new evidence has been revealed proving that Bonny was wrongfully accused of piracy. Instead, she was held as a hostage against her will by John Rackham and his pirate crew aboard the ship known as *The Vanity*. After learning of this new evidence, it is the decision of the court to exonerate Anne Bonny of all crimes and she will be granted a full pardon by the authority of Governor Nicholas Lawes of Jamaica.

"Oh, and Rogers, I would like the pardon completed within a week's time. Anne will be released to the custody of her father Mister William Cormac. She will travel with him back to their home in Charles Towne. Send word to me as soon as the pardon is in place so I can inform Mister Cormac to retrieve his daughter from Port Royal. Agreed?"

"Agreed. ... I will do so under one condition. After being released, Anne Bonny will agree never to be seen on land or water in the Caribbean."

"Considering that Anne has spent a good deal of time in a Port Royal prison waiting to be hung the day after her child is born, I would think that this will not be a point of contention. I have no doubt she will agree to your terms."

Later that evening, as William Cormac dines, the innkeeper delivers a sealed envelope to his table. He quickly notices the distinctive royal blue monogram of Bayard's wax seal. Cormac takes in a deep breath as he uses a knife from his table as a letter opener. He holds the letter close to the candlelight and reads it.

Mister Cormac,

I have met with Governor Rogers and he has agreed to grant Anne a full pardon and to release her into your custody as early as a week from today. As soon as I hear word from the Governor that Anne's pardon is in place, I will contact you. You will need to charter a ship and sail to Port Royal, Jamaica where Anne is being held. All should be arranged for her release.

Respectfully,

Chidley Bayard.

Cormac sets the letter on the table, smiles and contentedly continues to eat his dinner.

Chapter Forty-Two

Freedom Ransomed

Two cells separate Anne and Mary. They pass the time by telling stories about their pasts and recalling the events that took place while sailing the high seas. They sing traditional folk songs that Anne learned growing up in Ireland and Charles Towne and the songs Mary learned growing up in England, as well as sea shanties they learned while sailing the oceans with their shipmates.

Late one night, Anne and Mary try to estimate the times when their children will be born. Based upon their figures, Mary should have her child close to a month before Anne. They talk about what will happen after their children are born.

Anne tells Mary, "We are living out an odd existence these final months. Waiting for our children to be born, knowing that directly after they enter this world, we will be put to death. I am sure they will be taken straight to an orphanage to be raised by strangers."

Mary pauses and responds, "I despise the thought that our children will be raised by some old hag in an orphanage. Have you thought about what name you will give your child?"

"Be it born male, I will name him Jack after his father. Be it born female, I will name her Anne after her mother."

"I will do the same, born male, he will be named Thomas and if born female, she will be named Mary."

Day after day, Anne and Mary tell each other of events that happened when they were children. One day, the jailer interrupts them as he walks down the stone hallway and stops at Anne's cell. He stares at her for a moment and says, "Lass, I am sure that being caged up in that cell for as long as you have makes you lonely and long for satisfaction."

"Indeed, but I am perfectly satisfied with the storytelling of my friend two cells from me. I don't seem to be longing for anything else."

"Lass, by satisfaction I do not mean the kind you get by talking to another lass. As a matter of fact no talking need take place."

To mock the jailer's not so subtle innuendos, Mary lets out a loud, "Ha!"

After hearing Mary's reaction, Anne smiles. She turns her

back to the jailer and begins walking slowly away from the cell door toward the back wall of her cell. "Jailer, if I should wake up one day and feel a burning desire to be satisfied the way you imply, you certainly would not be the one delivering the satisfaction."

"Lass, how can you know such things when you have not seen the object that would deliver your satisfaction?

Mary's voice shrieks, "Sweet Jesus ... an elephant seal lives in his trousers!"

Anne turns back toward her cell door to learn the meaning of what Mary has just said. Anne sees the jailer standing in the same spot he was in only a minute ago. She sees him grinning from ear to ear and notices that he is using his eyes and head to direct her attention downward. Anne suddenly notices what Mary meant by using the term 'elephant seal.' The jailer has exposed himself to Anne and Mary. Anne takes one look and laughs aloud. She tries to soften her reaction by placing her hand over her mouth, but has little success. Her laughter is contagious and causes Mary to begin laughing too.

Anne begins mocking the jailer. "What would possess you to present yourself this way? Surely you don't believe that this exhibition would drive me insane with lust ..."

The jailer's prideful expression turns into one of embarrassment and anger as he quickly tucks his appendage back into his trousers. He begins walking away from Anne and Mary as they continue laughing. Anne grabs the steel bars of her cell door and places her face between them. "Jailer, it will be best for you to not harbor ideas of surprising us while we sleep. If you enter our cells, you will surely lose your Willy to a swift yank or chomp. It would be terribly embarrassing to have to explain to the guv-nah how you and your Willy were permanently separated."

Two weeks later, Anne is awakened by the echoing sound of Mary coughing in the middle of the night. "Mary, are you ill?"

"Anne, I cannot cool myself."

As the days pass, Mary's health continues to worsen. Anne tries to comfort Mary but feels helpless trying to send her comfort from two cells away. Mary begins to complain that a red rash is appearing all over her body.

Anne yells through her cell bars, down the hall to where the jailers all gather. "Jailer, you must fetch a physician; Mary is terribly ill."

The jailer walks down the hall, giving Anne a snarling look as he passes her cell. He continues to Mary's cell, stops, and shakes his keys loudly. Mary is lying in a fetal position on the wooden platform covered with hay that serves as her bed. He rattles his keys once more. Mary slowly lifts her head and whispers, "What the hell do you want?"

The jailer lets out a sarcastic jeer, and yelling down the hall to Anne, "Lass, you are right, she looks bloody awful."

Mary spits back in a weakened voice, "Bugger-off elephant seal!" She rolls over on her side, turning her back to the jailer, and falls back to sleep.

The jailer walks back down the hall to Anne's cell. "Physician? How do you expect to pay a physician's fee when you are locked away in a prison cell? I would reckon that you have nothing to pay him with. To have a physician see a condemned woman would take at least a quid, maybe two. Though, I might be able to fetch a physician if you make a payment to me ..."

Mary is in and out of consciousness but hears the jailer's proposition. She musters up enough strength to say, "Damn you Anne, you will not allow that hog to do what he wants with you. I will feel better soon enough."

The very thought of having the jailer's filthy body on top of her disgusts Anne to no end, but her love for Mary is too strong. She will do whatever it takes to cure her of the illness she is battling. In an effort to accept what she must do, Anne disconnects herself from the thought of having sex with the jailer. She thinks that if she can minimize the act in her mind, *it might be bearable if it means curing Mary.* She looks at the jailer and says, "I will agree to your terms, but only after you fetch a physician and she is treated. You will have one time with me and that's all! You will visit me at the darkest time of night, so that I have the benefit of darkness to keep you from my sight."

"Aye lass, I will fetch a physician for her, and it does not matter to me how dark it will be when I come for payment ..."

The next morning Anne calls out, "Mary, the physician will soon be here. He will cure you. You will be yourself in no time at all."

Mary does not respond to Anne. All is silent. Anne, in a panic, screams, "Mary, answer me!" Again, there's only silence. She sinks to the cell floor. Her heart breaks at the realization that Mary and her child are dead.

Anne cries out frantically, "Mary! Answer me! Please! Why are you not answering me?"

Anne stares into nothingness as tears overflow from her eyes.

Thirty minutes later, the jailer enters the prison with the physician. As he passes Anne's cell, he sees a heartbroken Anne sitting on the floor with her back against the wall, staring into space with her eyes red and swollen from crying. He does not say anything as he passes her. He leads the physician to Mary's cell, saying, "Here we are." The sound of the cell door is heard as it opens.

Anne hears the physician speak to Mary, "Love, I will need you to sit up to allow me to examine you." He sounds concerned. "Lass, can you hear me?" The lack of a response confirms to Anne that Mary is gone. She hears the physician say, "It seems that she has passed. See the red rash about her skin? I would diagnose that she perished due to complications from scarlet fever. For the safety of others, you should have the body removed immediately and burned."

Minutes later, Anne hears as the jailer removes Mary's

lifeless body from her cell and onto a wooden cart. As she is wheeled down the corridor, Anne sees that Mary lies on her back. At the moment the cart passes, its wheel hits a depression in the stone floor and jostles Mary's body, causing her head to turn toward Anne. Mary's eyes are open and it seems she deliberately turns her head to bid Anne a final farewell.

She whispers, "Good bye, Mary, I love you," and lets out a loud and sorrowful yell.

After Mary's death, time passes slowly. Anne becomes despondent. She does not eat, and her body begins to weaken. The jailer continually sees Anne in her depressed state and never approaches her for the payment she promised for fetching the physician.

Several days after Mary's passing, Anne hears the footfalls of two soldiers echo down the prison corridor, and gaining volume as they approach her cell. They come to a sudden stop. She hears one of the soldiers say, "Here she is, guv-nuh." She has run a high fever for days and been in and out of consciousness. Lying on her straw bed with her back to the cell door, she hears the guard say, "Well, all right, then." She hears the clinking of steel keys and realizes that this could mean that her fate is to stand on top of the gallows this day. She is delirious and does not consider that she has not yet had her child. She has been imprisoned for over three months. Knowing that Jack and the others are all gone, she has resigned herself to the ending that they faced.

The cell door creaks as it is opened. Anne lifts her

weakened body and turns her head. She looks at the cell floor, holds her arms outward and puts her hands together offering them to the guard for the iron shackles. She suddenly hears a familiar voice. "Annie ..."

At this moment, she realizes that only two people on this earth have ever called her "Annie." She looks up to see her father's face. Offering a slightly sympathetic smile, as if to provide comfort, he says, "Let's go home."

Anne sits deep in thought on the deck of her father's chartered ship as it sails from Port Royal. En route to Charles Towne, the ship passes the mouth of the harbor, when her thoughts are interrupted by one of the ship's crew, "Farewell, ye rogue." Anne looks toward a rocky point to see Jack's tar-covered body, caged and hanging on display. She does not look away until the island disappears from sight.

Later that evening, Anne's father tells her, "Word came to me that you were incarcerated in Jamaica." Cormac does not tell Anne that it was James who came to inform him of the news. "I chartered a ship to set sail for New Providence, where I contacted a gentleman I felt could influence your release. Coincidentally, this man said that the two of you know each other."

"This man said that we know each other? Father, what is his name?"

"His name is Chidley Bayard."

CHAPTER FORTY-THREE

HOMEWARD BOUND

Everyone is certain that Ajani has been lost to the sea after witnessing him being wounded and falling overboard during the British artillery barrage on *The Vanity*.

Now, a merchant ship sails away from a familiar coast on a sunny and windy day. A man is on the shore waving to the ship as it heads out to sea. He turns away from the ship and looks to the large expanse of land in front of him. As the sun is setting over the African countryside, he steps off the sandy beach and begins walking through tall waving grass. Ajani kneels to one knee, fills his hand with earth, and lets it sift through his fingers. Ajani is home, once again. He takes a deep breath, as if to welcome himself back to his homeland, pulls his bag of belongings tighter to his shoulder, and begins to walk inland.

Chapter Forty-Four

Reflection

Years later, Anne walks along a beach on an overcast and breezy day, wearing a dark dress and a wrap over her shoulders, she looks out toward the ocean. She listens to the sound of waves gently washing onto the Virginia shore.

Anne thinks to herself, *I often try to remember the faces of the men I sailed with. Many have faded from my memory. However, sometimes, when walking in the market, I believe I see the faces of those I once knew. I remember them as they were and not how they would be today. I yearn to call out their names, but hold my tongue. I know that they all have left this earth long ago. I often see Mary's face. How I miss her. Our souls were connected. I have never found another person I have been closer to. I have cheated, stolen, lied, and killed. The older I become, the more I ponder whether the debt I owe for my past sins is far too great to outweigh any forgiveness for the good life I've led since leaving New Providence so many years ago. Will I be forgiven?*

Anne's thoughts are interrupted by the sounds of children playing in the background. She turns and sees her husband smiling at her. She looks at her two young boys, John and William, chasing each other around the small sand dunes. Their playful sound is suddenly replaced by the sound of one of them yelling out in pain and then crying. Anne looks toward her children and sees her husband grabbing a wooden toy sword from her third child and, hears him scold, "Annie, you mustn't play so roughly with your brothers." Anne smiles and turns her head back to the sea.

A large Navy sloop comes into view at a distance, skirting the colonial shoreline and sailing south. Anne's eyes follow the ship as it passes, some three-hundred yards offshore. In a quiet voice she says, "Must be over two-hundred tons." Her husband heard her say something, but he could not make out what she said and asks, "What's that Anne?" Without taking her eyes off the passing ship, she turns her head slightly to the side and replies, "Nothing, I was only thinking aloud." She refocuses her attention back on the passing ship. A brisk breeze kicks up, causing Anne to adjust her wrap. She hears the faint voice of the ship's quartermaster issuing orders to his crew.

The breeze blows stronger as the sun briefly breaks from the clouds, casting light onto the water and shoreline. Looking upward to the sky, she sees a seagull gliding. The gull dips its wings, lands ten feet from her, and squawks. Anne looks back at the passing ship, as she slightly raises one corner of her mouth in a defiant grin.

THE END

ABOUT THE AUTHOR

Stephen Utley was born in Gary, Indiana in 1963. In the mid-70's his family relocated from Chicago, Illinois to Dallas, Texas where he resides today.

Having been aware that he was an artist from early on, his parents supported him in the pursuit of what was to become his calling: a career in the creative arts. After receiving his degree in commercial arts and advertising from TSTC in 1989, Steve served as creative director and president of Quill Advertising, a Dallas-based integrated communications firm. More recently, highlighting his talent and skill in graphic design and communications, Utley Creative Group was formed. Also based in Dallas, this virtual, creative firm is the latest project in his career spanning 25 years and covering all aspects of business-to-business and consumer-based marketing.

Steve is currently at work on his second book (working title: PEAK XV) which takes place in England and Nepal.

15998427R00188

Made in the USA
Charleston, SC
30 November 2012